# THE ART AND PRACTICE OF INVESTMENT

BY THE SAME AUTHOR

Purposeful Investment
Principles of Pension Fund Investment
Investment for All

# THE ART & PRACTICE OF INVESTMENT

WILLIAM G. NURSAW
F.C.I.S., A.C.I.I., F.S.S., F.I.Arb.
*Member of Society of Investment Analysts*

HUTCHINSON OF LONDON

Hutchinson & Co. (*Publishers*) Ltd
*3 Fitzroy Square, London W1*

London Melbourne Sydney Auckland
Wellington Johannesburg Cape Town
and agencies throughout the world

*First published March 1963*
*Second impression April 1963*
*Supplement March 1966*
*Second (revised) edition November 1967*
*Fourth impression February 1970*
*Third (revised) edition 1974*





*Set in Monotype Times Roman*

*Printed in Great Britain by*
*Ebenezer Baylis & Son Ltd, The Trinity Press*
*Worcester, and London, and bound by*
*Wm. Brendon & Son Ltd, Tiptree, Essex*

ISBN 0 09 120080 6 (cased)
0 09 120081 4 (paper)

*To the late*

SIDNEY JAMES PERRY, F.I.A.

*a pioneering stockbroker*

# Acknowledgements

To the many who have in a variety of ways helped this book along through its various impressions and editions and in particular to Peter Cramb, B.A. (Hons.), Queen's College, Oxford, specializing in portfolio management with a leading firm of stockbrokers, without whose help with the multiplicity of figures and in other ways I would never have successfully met my dateline for the third edition.

# Contents

# Preface to the Third Edition

No one need get dull practising the art of investment. One look at the Himalayan peaks and ravines pattern of the equity and government indices on pages 18 and 19 demonstrates this.

All indices, percentages and yields, indeed every figure, hundreds of them, were updated and the book completely revised when this edition went to press. At page proof stage (mid February 1974) many figures could unnecessarily have been altered – figures can get out of date in a week. They are only illustrative anyway. It is the principles that dominate and matter.

Very true, the investment scene is at present undergoing heavy bombardment mainly because of political uncertainties which have boiled over during the last two months: the miners' strike; the A.S.L.E.F. go slow; the dramatic rise in the price of oil; the three-day week; a massive deficit in our balance of payments; inflation and the Bank of England minimum lending rate has been as high as 13% with the local authorities having to pay as much as 17% for 7 day money.

Now we have a minority Labour Government with its first Budget announced literally a few hours before the book goes to press, with many items affecting investment – the basic income tax rate goes up to 33% from 30% but fortunately Advance Corporation Tax (p. 101) similarly increased – the top rate on earned income, now 83%, and 98% (p. 113) for persons who additionally have investment income in excess of £2000 per annum – stamp duty (p. 34) on share transfers doubled at 2% – Corporation Tax fixed at 52½% instead of the expected 50% (p. 102) – the 25% surrender of the investment dollar premium on a sale (p. 67) extended to all overseas currencies – infants' income added to the parents' income for tax purposes from 5th April, 1975 – the favourable tax advantages (p. 80) enjoyed by guaranteed income bonds ended for bonds issued after Budget Day – severe restrictions imposed on interest on borrowing as a charge against personal taxation – a gift tax to be payable on gifts made after Budget Day and a wealth tax to be introduced, details of both to be announced later; the former will doubtless end the seven-year estate duty waiting period (p. 117).

As a result the F.T. Industrial Share Index fell to an eleven-year low of 281·3. Nevertheless I see no reason for making any adjustment to what I have written. In a sentence, it has all happened before. Perhaps my chapter on the pressure on Stock Exchange investments will convince readers that we shall get back to normal, remembering that when the Social Security Act (1973) gets going there will be an extra almost £1000 million per annum looking for an investment home.

As I have stressed in the First Edition and in subsequent editions and impressions the art of investment can only be intelligently practised in the setting of a capitalist society, admittedly where the rewards, in a moving process which can be seen, are more and more equitably shared between capital, labour and the state through taxation for the common good. I believe that the large majority will continue to feel that we have the best basis for a society and that before long we will solve our problems to the satisfaction of that majority.

Consequently in these last months the equity and British Government 20 year bond indices have suffered heavy falls, as follows:

| | *8th February 1974* | *31st October 1973* |
|---|---|---|
| F.T. Industrial Share Index | 307·3 | 432·3 |
| F.T/A 651 All Share Index | 150·33 | 186·83 |
| F.T/A 20 year Government Bond Index | 52·38 | 62·80 |

WILLIAM G. NURSAW

# Introduction

FIRST a few words about how this book came to be written. Towards the end of 1960 I was invited to write a Paper for the 1961 Conference of the Chartered Institute of Secretaries on the subject of Investments in Trust, a review of Problems and Policies.

The more I got down to my task the more I became struck with the magnitude of the subject and in the end the Paper became the longest ever presented at the Annual Institute Conference. It was circulated beforehand both to the Press and to Institute members attending the conference and I introduced the Paper on 13th May, 1961 at the Royal Pavilion, Brighton. Much to my surprise and gratification, the Paper was acclaimed by the whole of the Financial Press while the *Annual Report* of the Chartered Institute of Secretaries referred to it as a 'best seller'. And out of the Paper has grown this book.

One of the problems has been the exceedingly heavy work involved in keeping prices, yields, and figures generally up to date. Up-to-the-minute figures are not, of course, fundamental to a book on investments. What matter above all else are the establishment and examination of the canons of investment and the gathering together of accumulated investment experience. However, these figures are as up to date as a publisher's time-table will allow.

The subject of investments is an intricate and specialized one. I have tried therefore to write in a clear manner, free from jargon, which will be understandable to the student and layman and at the same time stimulating and thought-provoking to the professional.

Investment covers a vast field and, although I am restricting my observations to stock exchange investments, I am still left with a formidable task. I propose:

(1) To give some indication of the total availability of stock exchange investments.
(2) To consider the extent to which the trustees of the various groups of trusts and others make use of stock exchange investments – that is, the pressure on these investments.

(3) To explore what I will call the science or art of investment as it affects the two main groups – fixed interest stocks and equities – to reflect upon the problems and the policies and, if possible, to formulate some conclusions.

(4) To consider the practice of investing in equity shares through (a) investment trusts and (b) unit trusts.

(5) To deal with the more important groups of trusts which look to stock exchange investments to provide the bulk of their investments and to consider the particular problems of these trusts and possible solutions: here I have in mind:
 (a) personal and family trusts;
 (b) pension funds;
 (c) charitable funds;
 (d) quasi trusts such as life assurance funds;
 (e) the field of investment advice generally, and
 (f) management of the personal funds of individuals.

(6) Finally, to mention the nature and effect of the Trustee Investment Act, 1961, not only upon trustees but upon the art of investment generally.

With the Second Edition and subsequent impressions the book has been issued in both hardback and paperback form, and the latter has been welcomed by the rapidly growing number of students who are studying for their professional examinations. The Stock Exchange which lists *The Art and Practice of Investment* among its recommended books recently extended its own examination to persons who are not employees of member firms.

There is an enormous growth of interest in investment by the so-called 'layman' through the family finance pages of the national press, including of course the *Guardian* for whom I have been writing on investment and insurance for over six years, following the four years I wrote for the *Observer*.

Since the book was first published eleven years ago I have added fifty per cent to the text (this time another twenty-one pages) but I have continued to restrict myself to Stock Exchange investments in some depth. If readers want to know my views on other types of investment (life assurance in its many forms, property, mortgages, house purchase, seven-year covenants, bonds in variety, overseas investment) they are set out in my book entitled *Investment for All.*

PART 1

# Availability of and Pressure on Stock Exchange Investments

## CHAPTER 1

# Availability of Stock Exchange Investments

To begin with I tried to ascertain the nominal and market values in total for the investments quoted on the London Stock Exchange and the twenty-two provincial stock exchanges. Securing figures for the latter was not simple and it was complicated by the fact that many securities are quoted on more than one stock exchange. I came to the conclusion that my purpose would be served if I used the very helpful figures which are quoted by the London Stock Exchange. I append, now, the latest figures quoted – namely those for the year ended 31st March, 1973. I have added the depreciation percentage for fixed-interest stocks. It will be noted that there are 8,960 investments quoted on the London Stock Exchange with a nominal value of £59,635,501,000 and a market value of £167,289,758,000.

The investments are grouped as follows:

TABLE 1

| | *No. of invest-ments* | *Nominal amount* £ | *Market values* £ | *Depreci-ation* % |
|---|---|---|---|---|
| (1) British Funds, etc. – British Government .. .. | 46 | 25,768,150,000 | 19,324,841,000 | 25·0 |
| (2) do. Guaranteed and Nationalisation Stocks .. .. | 14 | 1,039,020,000 | 725,578,000 | 30·2 |
| (3) do. N. Ireland Loan Stocks .. | 4 | 54,000,000 | 42,450,000 | 21·4 |
| (4) Corporation and County Stocks – Great Britain and N. Ireland .. .. .. | 768 | 2,004,121,000 | 1,696,130,000 | 15·4 |
| (5) Public Boards, etc. – Great Britain and N. Ireland .. | 81 | 348,947,000 | 249,491,000 | 28·5 |
| (6) Commonwealth Government and Provincial Securities | 103 | 571,656,000 | 428,710,000 | 25·0 |
| (7) Commonwealth Corporation Stocks .. .. .. | 11 | 18,453,000 | 14,753,000 | 20·1 |
| (8) Foreign Stocks, Bonds, etc. | 369 | 2,758,106,000 | 2,307,458,000 | 16·3 |
| (9) Corporation Stocks – Foreign .. .. .. | 45 | 58,855,000 | 25,695,000 | 56·3 |
| (10) Loan Capital .. .. .. | 2,567 | 7,170,156,000 | 5,901,341,000 | 17·7 |
| (11) Preference and Preferred Capital .. .. .. | 1,611 | 1,279,540,000 | 812,920,000 | 36·5 |
| (12) Ordinary and Deferred Capital .. .. .. | 3,312 | 18,564,497,000 | 130,366,670,000 | — |
| (13) Shares of no Par Value .. | 29 | — | 5,393,721,000 | — |
| | 8,960 | 59,635,501,000 | 167,289,758,000 | |

Taking the twenty-one-year period ending 31st March, 1973, the nominal and market values of all stocks quoted on the London Stock Exchange are detailed below:

TABLE 2

| *Year ended* | *Nominal values* £ | *Market values* £ | Financial Times *Indices* *Gilts* | *Fixed interest* | *Industrial* |
|---|---|---|---|---|---|
| 31st March, 1953 .. | 25,623,858,629 | 27,130,468,464 | 96·14 | 107·10 | 123·3 |
| 31st March, 1954 .. | 26,653,126,011 | 30,503,221,012 | 101·41 | 112·58 | 138·9 |
| 31st March, 1955 .. | 27,749,159,273 | 33,796,351,830 | 99·93 | 109·89 | 181·9 |
| 31st March, 1956 .. | 28,852,615,940 | 33,633,269,887 | 86·50 | 96·04 | 180·1 |
| 31st March, 1957 .. | 29,674,715,813 | 35,794,453,143 | 87·18 | 95·56 | 189·8 |
| 31st March, 1958 .. | 30,126,916,906 | 33,101,815,616 | 81·53 | 88·99 | 164·5 |
| 31st March, 1959 .. | 30,503,139,402 | 39,020,461,388 | 85·84 | 93·58 | 219·4 |
| 31st March, 1960 .. | 31,292,768,886 | 45,068,174,830 | 82·17 | 92·13 | 321·2 |
| 31st March, 1961 .. | 33,332,489,385 | 50,951,363,550 | 78·25 | 85·86 | 342·2 |
| 31st March, 1962 .. | 33,620,518,115 | 50,223,580,402 | 77·64 | 85·46 | 291·8 |
| 31st March, 1963 .. | 35,737,829,193 | 55,309,110,100 | 83·54 | 90·30 | 307·6 |
| 31st March, 1964 .. | 37,696,399,778 | 59,841,170,263 | 83·81 | 89·98 | 339·6 |
| 31st March, 1965 .. | 39,168,280,731 | 75,154,668,343 | 78·36 | 84·84 | 339·1 |
| 31st March, 1966 .. | 40,213,911,136 | 78,163,829,766 | 77·29 | 84·28 | 344·9 |
| 31st March, 1967 .. | 43,618,271,351 | 82,033,466,228 | 80·80 | 88·44 | 325·8 |
| 31st March, 1968 .. | 45,140,889,141 | 103,330,691,365 | 76·40 | 85·03 | 442·2 |
| 31st March, 1969 .. | 46,527,757,812 | 131,678,611,255 | 68·16 | 74·55 | 474·6 |
| 31st March, 1970 .. | 48,695,758,386 | 120,040,417,553 | 71·81 | 74·53 | 396·6 |
| 31st March, 1971 .. | 50,806,906,735 | 120,504,165,157 | 73·62 | 72·35 | 347·2 |
| 31st March, 1972 .. | 54,326,792,000 | 149,531,323,000 | 78·89 | 80·39 | 509·0 |
| 31st March, 1973 .. | 59,635,501,000 | 167,289,758,000 | 69·78 | 70·42 | 456·3 |

In order to indicate the effect of changes in market values I have added the *Financial Times* indices for the appropriate dates. It will be noted that the twenty-one years' average growth in nominal values is £1,701 million and in market values £7,008 million. As regards the latter, the industrial share index clearly shows that much of the increase in market values during the last fifteen years is due to the appreciation in the value of ordinary shares.

Similarly it will be of interest also to give details as at 31st March, 1973, of all equities quoted on the London Stock Exchange under their normal groupings. It will be noted that the figures cover 3,341 equities with nominal values of £18,564,497,000 and with market values of £135,760,391,000. (See Table 3.)

Over a period of seven years the number of quoted equities has fallen from 4,045 to 3,341, demonstrating the extent of takeovers and mergers during the period.

TABLE 3

| | *No. of securities* | *Nominal amount* £ | *Market valuation* £ |
|---|---|---|---|
| RAILWAYS – U.K. and other Commonwealth | 5 | 153,246,000 | 623,713,000 |
| ,, American .. | 2 | 28,925,000 | 7,400,000 |
| ,, Foreign .. | 6 | 21,314,000 | 5,426,000 |
| BANKS AND DISCOUNT COMPANIES .. .. .. | 84 | 1,853,091,000 | 12,327,665,000 |
| BREWERIES AND DISTILLERIES .. | 51 | 615,164,000 | 2,239,704,000 |
| CANALS AND DOCKS .. .. | 8 | 15,339,000 | 31,362,000 |
| COMMERCIAL, INDUSTRIAL, ETC. | 2,009 | 8,954,247,000 | 76,653,808,000 |
| ELECTRIC LIGHTING AND POWER .. .. .. | 9 | 23,566,000 | 308,434,000 |
| FINANCIAL TRUSTS, LAND, ETC. | 117 | 431,774,000 | 1,925,241,000 |
| GAS .. .. .. .. | 2 | 18,826,000 | 105,472,000 |
| INSURANCE .. .. .. | 46 | 315,600,000 | 3,276,550,000 |
| INVESTMENT AND UNIT TRUSTS | 367 | 1,589,396,000 | 6,021,681,000 |
| IRON, COAL AND STEEL .. | 29 | 433,951,000 | 1,265,075,000 |
| MINES – Australian .. .. | 14 | 211,535,000 | 1,036,885,000 |
| ,, Miscellaneous .. | 49 | 182,553,000 | 1,739,701,000 |
| ,, Rhodesian and East African .. .. | 19 | 112,436,000 | 316,271,000 |
| ,, South African .. | 96 | 396,741,000 | 4,336,784,000 |
| ,, West African .. | 8 | 4,558,000 | 4,363,000 |
| ,, Diamond .. .. | 8 | 24,886,000 | 1,866,965,000 |
| OIL .. .. .. .. | 26 | 2,242,155,000 | 16,820,776,000 |
| PROPERTY .. .. .. | 144 | 466,633,000 | 2,377,507,000 |
| RUBBER.. .. .. .. | 64 | 64,533,000 | 339,932,000 |
| SHIPPING .. .. .. | 29 | 154,626,000 | 643,708,000 |
| TEA AND COFFEE .. .. | 76 | 39,700,000 | 35,029,000 |
| TELEGRAPHS AND TELEPHONES | 4 | 164,496,000 | 1,422,735,000 |
| TRAMWAYS AND OMNIBUS .. | 7 | 7,805,000 | 10,517,000 |
| WATER WORKS .. .. | 62 | 37,401,000 | 17,687,000 |
| | 3,341 | 18,564,497,000 | 135,760,391,000 |

These figures include the market values of 25 no par value shares to a value of £5,393,771,000, which obviously cannot be given a nominal value.

*'Growth in Equities'*

Here are the figures from 1954, the first year they were made available, and for the following twenty years together with the *Financial Times* Industrial Share Index for each year.

TABLE 4

| *Year to 31st March* | (*a*) *Nominal value* £m. | (*b*) *Market value* £m. | Financial Times *Industrial Index* |
|---|---|---|---|
| 1954 | 3,475 | 10,543 | 138·9 |
| 1955 | 4,169 | 14,186 | 181·9 |

| | | | |
|---|---|---|---|
| 1956 | 4,548 | 15,295 | 180·1 |
| 1957 | 4,897 | 16,905 | 189·8 |
| 1958 | 5,280 | 14,958 | 164·5 |
| 1959 | 5,880 | 20,186 | 219·4 |
| 1960 | 6,610 | 26,567 | 321·2 |
| 1961 | 7,371 | 31,763 | 342·2 |
| 1962 | 8,240 | 31,609 | 291·8 |
| 1963 | 8,766 | 33,951 | 307·6 |
| 1964 | 9,989 | 37,955 | 339·6 |
| 1965 | 11,318 | 53,819 | 339·1 |
| 1966 | 11,581 | 56,261 | 344·9 |
| 1967 | 12,260 | 56,763 | 325·8 |
| 1968 | 12,845 | 78,133 | 442·2 |
| 1969 | 14,174 | 108,255 | 474·6 |
| 1970 | 15,079 | 94,928 | 396·6 |
| 1971 | 15,508 | 94,104 | 347·2 |
| 1972 | 15,784 | 116,896 | 509·0 |
| 1973 | 18,564 | 135,760 | 456·3 |

Clearly, in considering the availability of equity shares, it will be noted that much of the growth is due to the appreciation in market values as indicated by the *Financial Times* index figures.

In considering the figures of Table 1 (page 3) it must be borne in mind that there is a not inconsiderable amount of double counting in the case of both fixed-interest and equity stocks. I refer to the investments which appear in the balance sheets of:

(a) the banks;
(b) insurance companies;
(c) the investment trusts;
(d) the investments of the unit trusts;
(e) the large blocks of shares held by holding companies and controlling companies; and
(f) the investments generally held by joint stock companies.

There is plenty of scope for research, if reasonably accurate figures are required, on a scale which I am unable to undertake; but the following is of interest:

Unit trusts have some £2,000 million in equities.

Insurance companies have over £4,500 million (book values) invested in equities – market values could be estimated at more than £7,500 million.

On a conservative estimate, investment trusts have £4,500 million invested in British equities.

Pension funds must have over £6,400 million in equities and have caught up with insurance companies.

There is also some additional double counting in investment trusts themselves, inasmuch as at least £300 million is invested by investment trusts in investment trusts.

These figures will serve to emphasize the point I am making – namely, that the availability of equity shares in particular is a good deal less than it appears to be.

CHAPTER 2

# Pressures on Stock Exchange Investments

HERE again there is scope for lengthy research and I am unable to give reliable figures, but I have been able to unearth what I hope will be thought to be some interesting information which will assist in giving an overall picture.

*Insurance Companies*

The funds of the insurance companies are in excess of £18,500 million, of which over £12,000 million are probably invested in stock exchange securities. The estimated annual growth of these funds is £1,500 million, and £1,000 million may well be invested annually in stock exchange securities, with perhaps approximately £500 million going into equity stocks.

*Pension Funds*

According to statistics published by the Central Statistical Office, superannuation and pension funds, including local authority superannuation funds, may be estimated at over £11,000 million, and of these over £9,000 million are invested in stock exchange securities. It is estimated that these funds are growing at the rate of over £900 million per annum, with an annual pressure of over £550 million on stock exchange securities, of which probably over £400 million found its way into equities in 1972. Other things being equal, more will have gone into equities in 1974 and subsequent years, particularly as some local authority superannuation funds previously limited to fixed-interest securities have still to catch up on the powers to buy equities given to them in the Trustee Investments Act, 1961.

*Unit Trusts*

Unit trust funds are in excess of £2,500 million and growing at the rate of £250 million per annum with the large bulk of their funds in equities at home and overseas.

*Investment Trusts*

I estimate that the investment trust movement supports the market with new money to the extent of £60 million per annum.

*Bank and Insurance Companies as Trustees*

It is estimated that banks and insurance companies, as trustees, held over £1,500 million in trust, of which £500 million were invested in gilt-edged securities alone. Obviously of the other £1,000 million a considerable portion would be invested in equities. No figures of the annual growth in the funds are given, but a modest growth of 3 per cent. will give £45 million per annum; it seems not unreasonable to estimate that more than half this growth will find its way into equities.

*Public Trustee*

It would appear from the latest annual report of the Public Trustee that funds under his care total approximately £305 million of which £260 million were probably invested in stock exchange securities with approximately £100 million in government securities, £160 million in the debentures, preference, and ordinary shares of industrial, commercial, and finance companies. The amount invested in equities probably totals approximately £150 million, which is an appreciable increase and demonstrates that the Public Trustee has made full use of his new powers under the Trustee Investments Act.

Unhappily, in my view, the office of the Public Trustee is to end in due course and new business is not being taken on, but it will take many years before he can transfer or wind up his existing trusts and executorships.

*Other Trust Funds*

There are no figures which begin to assess the funds held by individual trustees of family and other trusts, or by charities including the wealthy London Livery Companies for that matter. All that is known is that the Nathan Committee in its report on Charitable Trusts (December 1952) stated that 'because of lack of knowledge of what Charitable trusts there are, it is not possible to state what proportion of all available trust funds is vested in the official trustees, but the latest return presented shows the nominal value of the investments held (by the official trustees) on 71,142 accounts to exceed

116 million'. There is scope for almost a lifetime's research if reliable figures are to be obtained – the amount involved is colossal. There are further figures given in the chapter on charities (p. 127).

The Trustee Savings Bank Special Investment Department has over £900 million invested in quoted fixed-interest securities but no equities. The recently established Investment Account of the National Savings Bank (Post Office) is making good progress. The enlarged investment powers of the Trustee Investments Act, 1961 gave a fillip to equity investment and this is a continuing factor.

*Some Conclusions*

*Fixed-interest Stocks* – These have generally been out of favour since 1958 although there have been brief periods when they have been preferred to equities, particularly by insurance companies and pension funds. However, for most of the time investors have had to be encouraged by higher and higher interest rates to support this section of the market. It may not always be so, and I believe the time will come when fixed-interest stocks will feel the full pressure of investment demand. The supply then could be outstripped by demand.

*Equities* – With equities there has been great investment pressure over the last ten years or so – in fact, at times pressure has been terrific. This has been evidenced by the fantastic over-subscription of some equity issues. In 1973 one issue was 139 times over-subscribed.

At the time of writing, the equity market is under adverse pressures following the financial crisis of the pound and our adverse balance of payments position. Although the immediate prospects for equities do not appear to be good, there will, nevertheless, be intelligent buying of equities all the time and especially by the long-term institutional investor. Politics apart, I foresee heavy buying pressure on the equity market as soon as it becomes apparent that Britain is likely to solve its balance of payments problems and to maintain the status of sterling.

During recent years many of the larger trusts have had their investment powers extended by invoking the power of the Variation of Trusts Act, 1958. More than a few boroughs and municipal corporations have, as a result of private Acts of Parliament, taken powers to buy equities for their superannuation and other funds. These enlarged powers have been used. The Church Commissioners and many of the large charitable trusts have also gone heavily into equities. As mentioned earlier, the Trustee Investments Act, 1961 has also played its part on the pressures on equities – a continuing factor too, as it will take years for trustees, including trustees of pension funds, to obtain their full quota.

Clearly there is still scope for institutions and others to increase the proportion of their funds in equities. 'Lloyd's' some years ago departed from its 'all-Trustee' rule for deposits and now allows all the deposit to be invested in equities. The so-called 'man-in-the-street' has shown that he intends to ride on the equities band-wagon and has been buying equities either direct or through unit trusts.

Equities have been bought at prices higher than those current at the time of writing and although some trustees and other investors are licking their wounds, I have no doubt that in due course, *politics apart*, investors will be chasing equities back to prices appreciably above the high levels of May 1972.

The cult of the ordinary share has been in full swing for more than ten years, and it seems evident from a consideration of some of the apparently ridiculously low yields which have ruled at times (– or are they? – see later under investment analysis, page 54), which seems to discount not only the future but the hereafter also, that part of the appreciation in the value of ordinary shares has resulted from too much money chasing too little stock. Unless there is going to be some change in sentiment (a return to favour of gilts or a sustained lack of confidence in our industrial future) this pressure on ordinary shares will be maintained.

Finally, and as a matter of interest, an analysis of shareholdings in 1957 (see page 13) was undertaken as part of a large-scale investigation of the ownership and distribution of property in the United Kingdom on which Mr C. H. Feinsteen and Mr J. R. S. Revell researched at the University of Cambridge, Department of Applied Economics. The figures appended are most revealing.

In a book published on 24th November, 1966, *The Owners of Quoted Ordinary Shares – A survey for 1963* by J. R. S. Revell and John Moyle, the authors mention how this time they have gone behind the nominee holdings in getting at their scientific estimates of the spread of shareholdings. They also recalculated the 1957 figures. The comparative information is given as in the second table on page 13.

The most striking feature is the sharp drop in the ownership of shares by individual persons although the proportion is still high. It is not high, however, in terms of the 36 million adult population of Britain, as according to a survey made by the Stock Exchange in

1966 only 2½ millions, namely 7 per cent., invest directly on the Stock Exchange.

The figures were further updated to 31st December, 1969, in John Moyle's book, *The Pattern of Ordinary Share Ownership 1957/70*, published in 1971. The figures appear in column 3 of the table on page 13. The growth in institutional investment in equity shares is very marked.

## HOLDERS OF ORDINARY SHARES

(Market values at 1.7.57)

| *Holders* | *Aggregate holding* £m. | *Per cent. of total* |
|---|---|---|
| Insurance and assurance companies .. .. .. | 735 | 8·0 |
| U.K. banks and nominees[1] .. .. .. .. | 1,403 | 15·3 |
| Pension funds .. .. .. .. .. .. | 113 | 1·2 |
| Investment trusts[2] .. .. .. .. .. | 273 | 3·0 |
| Other financial institutions .. .. .. .. | 136 | 1·5 |
| Industrial and commercial companies .. .. | 186 | 2·0 |
| Charities, churches, etc.[3] .. .. .. .. | 118 | 1·3 |
| Overseas: (*a*) Holders resident outside U.K. .. | 394 | 4·3 |
| (*b*) Overseas banks and nominees .. | 53 | 0·6 |
| Executors and trustees[4] .. .. .. .. | 197 | 2·1 |
| Personal holdings .. .. .. .. .. | 5,102 | 55·6 |
| Not classified[5] .. .. .. .. .. .. | 465 | 5·1 |
| Total .. .. .. .. .. .. | 9,175 | 100·0 |

[1] Includes discount companies and all nominee companies except those of banks operating overseas.

[2] Only investment trusts quoted on London Stock Exchange.

[3] Charitable and educational organizations, Church Commissioners and religious organizations, learned and professional bodies, and London livery companies.

[4] Includes also the Public Trustee, Official Solicitor, and Accountant-General of the Supreme Court.

[5] Includes the British Government and social, political, and cultural organizations.

## BENEFICIAL OWNERS OF QUOTED ORDINARY SHARES

Percentages of total market value

| *Category of owner* | *1st July 1957** | *31st Dec. 1963* | *31st Dec. 1969* |
|---|---|---|---|
| Persons, executors and trustees .. | 65·8 | 54·0 | 47·4 |
| Insurance .. .. .. .. | 8·8 | 10·0 | 12·2 |
| Pension funds .. .. .. | 3·4 | 6·4 | 9·0 |
| Investment trusts .. .. .. | 5·2 | 7·4 | 7·6 |
| Unit trusts .. .. .. .. | 0·5 | 1·3 | 2·9 |
| Non-financial companies .. .. | 2·7 | 5·1 | 5·4 |
| Overseas residents .. .. .. | 4·4 | 7·0 | 6·6 |
| Other .. .. .. .. .. | 9·2 | 8·8 | 8·9 |
| | 100·0 | 100·0 | 100·0 |

* Recalculated.

PART 2

# The Art of Investment

## CHAPTER 3

# Fixed-Interest Stocks

*Introduction*

Investment can hardly yet be described as a science, although in many ways there are scientific approaches to investment. I feel it can best be described as an art.

The object of investment can be stated very simply. It is to secure the highest income and the highest capital appreciation in real terms of purchasing power. With this object reasonably assured, other objectives become secondary.

Broadly the investor and trustee is offered two main groups of Stock Exchange investment – fixed-interest stocks and equities – and he is offered a wide choice in each group. Subject to any limitation in his powers, a trustee can invest his fund wholly in the one or the other or in varying proportions of each. The owner of a fund having a free choice would do well to reflect on what the two main groups offer investment-wise. This may seem to state the obvious, but behind the right choice lies much applied investment skill.

*Fixed-interest Stocks*

As the name implies, these entitle the investor to a fixed rate of interest. They are broadly classified on page 3, items (1) to (11). There are two wide groups – irredeemable stocks and redeemable stocks. The former either can never be redeemed or are redeemable only at the option of the borrower – that is, when it suits him.

A redeemable stock is usually redeemable at par, with sometimes an option on the part of the borrower to redeem earlier but usually on more favourable paper terms to the stockholder; the option, however, is still against him, as he may want to retain his holdings. A redeemable stock is said to be 'dated', and dated stocks are roughly divided into three groups – short-, medium-, and long-dated. The advantage of such a stock is that the investor knows that he will be repaid at a price fixed at the time of the issue of the stock – assuming,

# Equity and Gilt-Edged Indices Charted 1925–1965

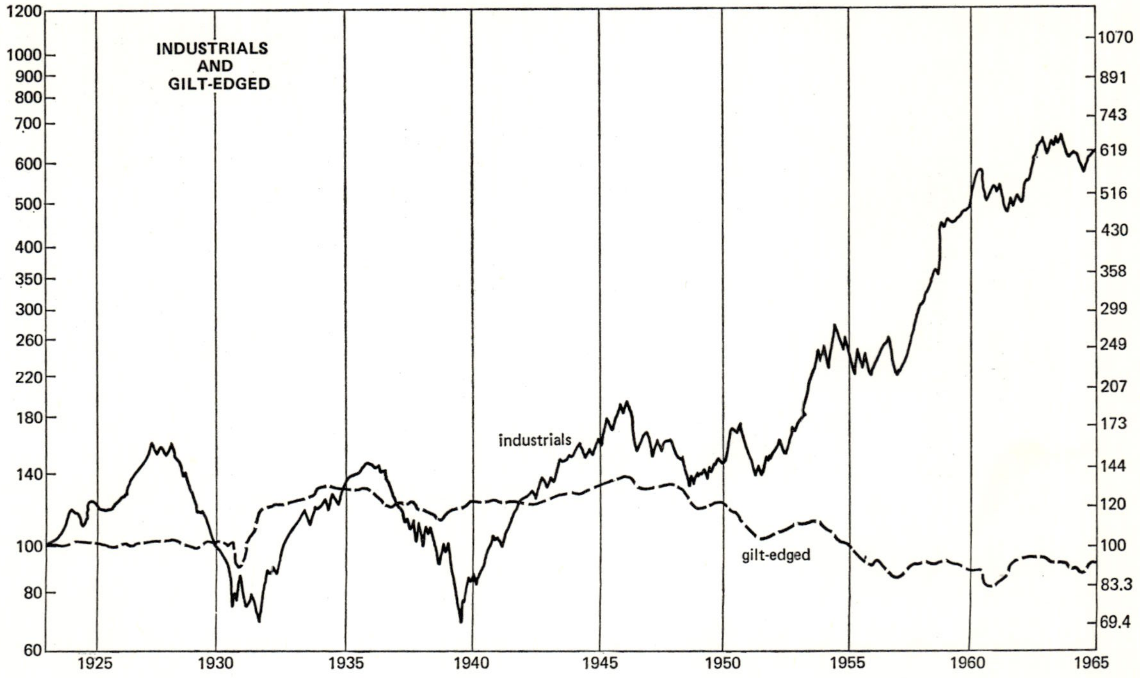


With acknowledgements to the *Investors' Chronicle*.

# Equity and Gilt-Edged Indices Charted 1949–1973

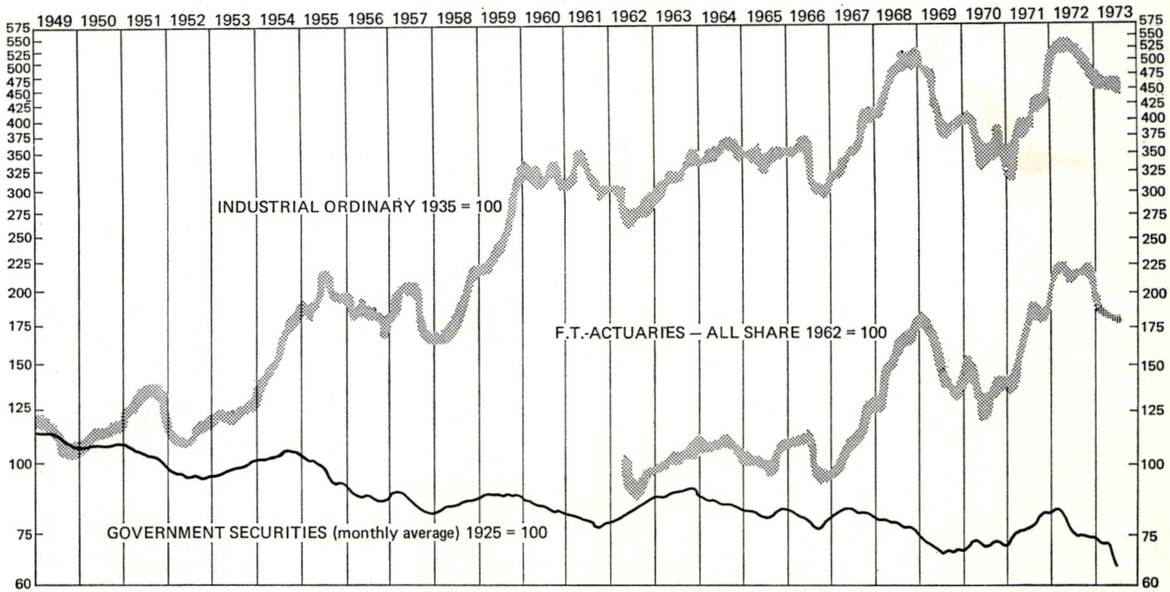


With acknowledgements to the *Financial Times*.

of course, he chooses a sound investment. Obviously, during the term of the stock the price will fluctuate with changes in current interest rates, and one of the problems which will engage the thoughts of the investor is whether he will be able to reinvest interest-wise as favourably when the stock is paid off.

Let me state here that although fixed-interest stocks seem to have all the appearance of security they have provided no protection against inflation. The gilt they earned during the late Victorian and Edwardian gold standard eras has unfortunately disappeared almost without a trace. But fixed-interest stocks are not without their uses and their day may well return. They are essential to some, if not most, portfolios. The selection of the right redemption date and the right fixed-interest stock is the best answer to an expected fixed liability or commitment.

Fixed-interest stocks, although clearly vulnerable to inflation, show less violent changes in value than equities, which, despite their excellent performance in the longer term, present the investor at times with simply appalling troughs of depressed prices. If there is any doubt of this, consider the graphs on pages 18 and 19, which compare gilts with industrials, and note the deep troughs and the lesser troughs.

In the case of redeemable stocks there are two yields to consider – the flat yield (so much money invested, so much annual income, the simple percentage interest yield) and the appropriate redemption yield. The latter is the yield which takes into account purchase price and maturity price and thus truly evaluates the interest rate, and it is probably the only yield to consider when the same people are interested in both the capital and income. It is the general practice to quote two redemption yields, the gross and the net.

*Some Comparative Yields on British Government Stocks*

Here are some British government stocks having various maturity dates. The same coupon has been selected for the purpose of comparison. The gross redemption yield is the yield to consider when the fund or investor is not liable to tax. The final column shows the net redemption yield grossed at 30 per cent. and shows what a fund or investor really earns when subject to tax at the basic rate of 30 per cent. The higher taxpayer does better still. It will be noted that as the term lengthens so the flat yield increases.

Currently the longest dated British government stock is $7\frac{3}{4}$ per cent. Treasury Stock 2012/15 with gross flat yield of £11·12 per cent.

and gross redemption yield of £11·17 per cent. Treasury 2½ per cent. stock was issued at 99½ by the late Dr Dalton, the Socialist Chancellor of the Exchequer. Its ensuing depreciation nearly wrecked trade unions' finances.

| *Stock* | *Dates* | *Price* | *Gross flat yield %* | *Gross redemption yield to final date* | *Net redemption yield grossed up** |
|---|---|---|---|---|---|
| | | | £ | £ | £ |
| 3% Savings Bonds .. | 1965–75 | 89½ | 3·35 | 8·73 | 11·12 |
| 3% Electricity Stock.. | 1974–77 | 83¼ | 3·60 | 8·45 | 10·47 |
| 3% Treasury Stock .. | 1979 | 73 | 4·18 | 9·09 | 11·30 |
| 3% Transport Stock.. | 1978–88 | 48⅜ | 6·23 | 9·62 | 11·67 |
| 3% Gas Stock .. | 1990–95 | 40¾ | 7·50 | 9·64 | 11·27 |
| And, by way of comparison, | | | | | |
| 2½% Treasury Stock.. | — | 23 | 11·27 | Redeemable at option of Brit. govt. in 1975 or after | |

* After income tax of 30%.

It will have been noted that the redeemable stocks quoted earlier have different redemption dates. This is a very short selection. Taking the whole field of fixed-interest stocks, it would probably be possible to plan a portfolio where a different stock is being paid off each year. To plan on this basis would certainly minimize the chances of the investor having a large proportion of a fund paid off at a time when reinvestment was unattractive owing to low interest rates.

I have already referred to the inflation risks of this type of security. If inflation is going to continue, something may have to be done by the Government (and others) to relate interest rates to real money values – say, to tie interest rates to the cost of living. This is not a fatuous suggestion. The Government gets its money and where it is invested in *public works* its underlying value grows in the real values which represent it. Indeed an issue was made in July 1965 by a relatively unknown company. It was referred to as an 8 per cent. Cost of Living Stock (Unsecured). It was issued at par and a few weeks later it had still kept its price. The terms of issue provided for a seven-year review of both the interest rate and the redemption price of the stock by reference to any rise in the cost of living as indicated in the Official Index of Retail Prices. The application of the formula could result in a maximum rate of interest of 10 per cent. and a maximum redemption price of £125.

There is for all practical purposes at the present time really little to choose between 7¾ per cent. Treasury Stock 2012/15 and Treasury 2½ per cent. Stock. The former is, for present-day considerations, virtually irredeemable, even though the Government has undertaken to redeem it by 2015. If interest rates in the next ten years fall appreciably, both stocks would show substantial appreciation. Irredeemable stocks have had few friends in recent years and at times tend to be under-valued. Irredeemable stocks when depressed in price are very suitable for permanent funds such as charitable and pension funds.

There is agitation from time to time to the effect that the Government should give a final redemption date to $3\frac{1}{2}$ per cent. War Loan (present price $32\frac{1}{4}$). Personally I can see no justification for this. It would probably be redeemed or, what amounts to the same thing, reach its par value if (and it's a big if) 3 per cent. became again the Government's borrowing rate for short and medium securities.

It will have been noted that maturity dates are an important factor in fixed-interest stock investment. Another is the rate of interest; there is the choice between two extremes – low and high coupon stocks or, to put it another way: maximum capital appreciation or maximum income? The high taxpayer wants capital appreciation and he can certainly get it if he chooses a low coupon short-dated British government stock. Take, for example, Treasury 3 per cent. Stock 1979: the flat gross yield at the current price of 73 is a mere £4·18 per cent. but the net redemption yield is £7·9 per cent. This is equivalent to a gross yield of approximately 58·6 per cent. if the investor pays tax at the highest rate of 90 per cent.

Before passing on to the various groups of fixed-interest stocks I would mention:

(1) It is an established axiom when purchasing fixed-interest stocks to buy long-dated stocks when interest rates are high and to buy short-dated stocks when interest rates are low. The investor has, of course, to be able to make up his mind when interest rates *are* high, and many an error has been made during the past fifteen years in thinking that interest rates were then high – only to find them go appreciably higher. Writing in *Investments in Trusts* early in 1961 I expressed the opinion, thus exposing myself to the same error, that interest rates were high then and would remain high. They have gone much higher than I ever contemplated; but I feel that rates will eventually come down, although not to the rates ruling at the time of the Dalton era.

(2) Where a stock has two redemption dates, the early one giving the borrower an option to repay on terms and the later one a

final repayment date, avoid choosing a stock where the gap is more than three to five years.

(3) Until October 1972 yields on fixed-interest stocks, particularly short- and medium-dated stocks, were influenced by the Bank Rate, and Bank Rate was used *sometimes*, albeit not particularly effectively, to control credit by increasing the cost of borrowing, or alternatively to expand the demand for credit by decreasing the cost of borrowing.

As a matter of history, here are the changes in the Bank Rate from 30th June, 1932 to the time it was abandoned.

| | % | | % |
|---|---|---|---|
| 30th June, 1932 | 2 | 2nd November, 1961 | 6 |
| 24th August, 1939 | 4 | 8th March, 1962 | 5½ |
| 28th September, 1939 | 3 | 22nd March, 1962 | 5 |
| 26th October, 1939 | 2 | 26th April, 1962 | 4½ |
| 8th November, 1951 | 2½ | 3rd January, 1963 | 4 |
| 11th March, 1952 | 4 | 27th February, 1964 | 5 |
| 17th September, 1953 | 3½ | 23rd November, 1964 | 7 |
| 13th May, 1954 | 3 | 3rd June, 1965 | 6 |
| 27th January, 1955 | 3½ | 14th July, 1966 | 7 |
| 24th February, 1955 | 4½ | 26th January, 1967 | 6½ |
| 16th February, 1956 | 5½ | 16th March, 1967 | 6 |
| 7th February, 1957 | 5 | 4th May, 1967 | 5½ |
| 19th September, 1957 | 7 | 19th October, 1967 | 6 |
| 20th March, 1958 | 6 | 9th November, 1967 | 6½ |
| 22nd May, 1958 | 5½ | 18th November, 1967 | 8 |
| 19th June, 1958 | 5 | 21st March, 1968 | 7½ |
| 14th August, 1958 | 4½ | 19th September, 1968 | 7 |
| 20th November, 1958 | 4 | 27th February, 1969 | 8 |
| 21st January, 1960 | 5 | 5th March, 1970 | 7½ |
| 23rd June, 1960 | 6 | 15th April, 1970 | 7 |
| 27th October, 1960 | 5½ | 1st April, 1971 | 6 |
| 8th December, 1960 | 5 | 2nd September, 1971 | 5 |
| 26th July, 1961 | 7 | 22nd June, 1972 | 6 |
| 5th October, 1961 | 6½ | | |

*Bank of England Minimum Lending Rate*

This replaced Bank Rate in October 1972. Announced every Friday, it is based on the average Treasury Bill rates plus ½ per cent. rounded up to the nearest ¼ per cent. The object, it seems, is to soften the repercussions following sharp changes in Bank Rate. Since its introduction the rate has varied between 7¼ per cent. (13th October, 1972) and 11½ per cent. (announced 27th July, 1973). Thus Bank Rate has, in effect, been almost doubled in just over a year without the drama associated with rises in Bank Rates of such traumatic dimensions.

CHAPTER 4

# Main Groups of Fixed-Interest Stocks

LET us examine the main types of *fixed-interest securities*. The figures quoted for the stocks are similar to those quoted on page 3.

British government stocks; corporation and county stock; public boards; dominion, provincial and colonial government and corporation stocks; industrial loan capital stocks including convertible loan stocks whilst unconverted are narrow-range investments under the Trustee Investment Act whereas convertible loan stocks (on conversion into equity shares); preference and preferred ordinary stocks are wider-range investments.

Foreign government stocks of any kind are excluded from either range.

*British Government Stocks*, including securities guaranteed by the British government (nominal value £26,807,170,000; market value £20,053,419,000). The importance of this group can be judged by the fact that in nominal values it represents over 44·19 per cent. of all securities quoted on the London Stock Exchange and, on a market value, nearly 12·3 per cent. Also 65·3 per cent. and 65·0 per cent. of the nominal and market values respectively of all fixed-interest stocks.

British government stocks have many advantages. No one has any fear that the interest will not be paid regularly, or that, in the case of a redeemable stock, the holders will not be given an opportunity of having cash on redemption (even though a conversion stock may be offered as an alternative) or that there will be any moratoria; further, there is always a ready market for the stock. If inflationary trends and politics over the years could be disregarded here is the perfect stock. Unfortunately neither can be disregarded, and investors have to make use of British government stocks intelligently, not abdicating their thinking by mere purchases of British government securities.

Inflation will crop up frequently in this book, and the dangers from this source are perhaps more readily assessable than risks of political interference. The Dalton period was a most unnatural epoch – to the expert, clearly fraught with danger; its effects are still with us. It completely upset the natural rise and fall of gilt-edged prices and produced a situation which still causes some investors to lick their wounds.

Despite the poor performance of British government securities in recent years, they had at one time a scarcity value. Until the statutory investment powers of trustees (hitherto governed by the Trustee Act, 1925) were extended by the Trustees Investments Act, 1961, British government securities were the main investments of trustees. This must have been worth a few points in value, and one wonders what has been the long-term effect on the value of British government securities as a result of trustees using and continuing to use their extended powers fully. One can only hope that favourable factors will emerge to offset this.

War Loan – particularly War Loan – and other British government securities are in a specially privileged position. Interest on $3\frac{1}{2}$ per cent. War Loan in registered form is paid gross and it is tax-free in the hands of non-residents of the United Kingdom. Interest on the following other British government stocks is tax-free in the hands of non-residents, but subject to the completion of the requisite forms by or on behalf of non-residents.

Treasury $5\frac{1}{2}$%, 1974
Treasury $6\frac{3}{4}$%, 1974
Treasury 6%, 1975
Treasury 8%, 1975
Savings 3%, 1965–75
Exchequer $6\frac{1}{2}$%, 1976
Treasury $6\frac{1}{2}$%, 1976
Victory 4% by 1st September, 1976
Treasury $6\frac{1}{4}$%, 1977
Treasury 9%, 1978
Exchequer 5%, 1976–78
Treasury 3%, 1979
Treasury 9%, Convertible 1980
Funding $5\frac{1}{4}$%, 1978–80
Treasury $8\frac{1}{2}$%, 1980–82
Funding $5\frac{1}{2}$%, 1982–86
Treasury $8\frac{1}{2}$%, 1984–86
Funding $6\frac{1}{2}$%, 1985–87
Treasury $7\frac{3}{4}$%, 1985–88
Treasury $8\frac{1}{4}$%, 1987–90
Funding $5\frac{3}{4}$%, 1987–91
Funding 6%, 1993
Treasury 9%, 1994
Treasury 9%, 1992–96
Treasury $8\frac{3}{4}$%, 1997
Treasury $6\frac{3}{4}$%, 1995–98
Treasury $9\frac{1}{2}$%, 1999
Treasury 8%, 2002–06
Treasury $5\frac{1}{2}$%, 2008–12
Treasury $7\frac{3}{4}$%, 2012–15

These stocks and $3\frac{1}{2}$ per cent. War Loan, if held by non-residents, are not subject to British estate duty – a further privilege.

*Corporation and County Stocks* (nominal value £2,004,121,000, market value £1,696,130,000). The amounts have nearly doubled in four years. These include the stocks issued by the county councils, the county boroughs, the local borough councils, and the like. They offer a slightly higher rate of interest than British government stocks of similar terms. The difference, however, is often not sufficient in my opinion to justify choosing a corporation stock in preference to a British government stock, especially as the former is not quite so marketable. Obviously, the borrowing status of the various county councils and boroughs will vary, and some corporations will be able to borrow on better terms than others. The majority were trustee securities under the Trustee Act, 1925.

*Corporations – Temporary Deposits and Mortgages* – Although not quoted on any stock exchange, it is appropriate here to mention corporation deposits and mortgages in which a large business has developed in the last ten years or so. The deposits, which are at competitive rates, are accepted by corporations for both modest and very large amounts on weekly call or for periods, ranking as temporary deposits up to a few years. Here are some examples of current rates:

| | % |
|---|---|
| Seven-day call money about .. | $8\frac{3}{4}$ |
| One month fixed .. .. .. | $9\frac{1}{2}$ |
| Three months fixed .. .. | $10\frac{3}{4}$ |
| Fixed for 364 days .. .. | $10\frac{3}{4}$ |
| Two-year Mortgages .. .. | $10\frac{3}{4}$ |

This is the pattern with interest rates at a high level. At the time the first edition went to press (November 1962) the figures were respectively, $4\frac{1}{4}$, $4\frac{1}{4}$, $4\frac{3}{8}$, 5 and 6.

At the time of revising this edition, short-term money rates were high all over the world and seemed to have found no ceiling. Indeed, I know of investment managers obtaining around 17 per cent. for money on seven days' call. These are all-time highs, and the same sort of conditions were operating in the United States. I feel that this cannot last and the time will come when more normal rates, say 5 per cent. for money on call, will come again.

*Public Boards, etc.* (nominal value £348,947,000; market value £249,491,000). This classification covers harbour and dock boards, port authorities, some water boards, etc. They give a yield slightly in excess of corporation stocks.

The status of public board stocks has suffered a reverse following the Government's decision not to underwrite the liabilities of the Mersey Docks & Harbour Board. The Board has thus been left to fend for itself and the likely result is a scheme of arrangement involving a serious writing down of the Board's loan and equity capital.

*Dominion, Provincial and Colonial Government and Corporation Stocks* (nominal value £590,109,000; market value £443,463,000). These amounts outstanding have steadily gone down over recent years with the larger Commonwealth countries seeking finance from the United States. Obviously this heading covers such diverse Commonwealth countries as Canada, Australia, Malaysia, Kenya, Jamaica, Nyasaland, and their corporation stocks. Clearly, some of the countries concerned would be able to borrow on more favourable terms than others, and naturally a differential in rates emerges as between the various stocks. The better stocks give an extra 50p per cent. yield over their British government counterparts.

*Foreign Government and Corporation Stocks* (nominal value £2,816,961,000; market value £2,333,153,000). The depreciation 17·2 per cent. should be noted, but it gives no real measure of what investors have really lost in this type of stock, since so many worthless stocks are no longer quoted. Fortunately – and is there not a lesson here – these were not included as authorized investments for trustees in the 1925 Act. As a group their investment record has been appalling, as in the case of British companies operating in certain foreign countries. Two world wars, repudiation of existing indebtedness by new regimes, the sequestration of property and national bankruptcies, have reduced to a handful the number of countries which have never given their foreign investors any anxiety.

*Industrial Loan Capital* (nominal value £7,170,156,000; market value £5,901,341,000). Up by over 100 per cent. in seven years. The term 'loan capital' normally covers prior charge stock, debentures, and convertible debentures – also unsecured loan stocks. Apart from British government stocks, debentures have always been favourite fixed-interest stocks of the institutional investor and the trustee with full investment powers. As a result, these stocks are tightly held and there is only a modest market in individual stocks. Now that all trustees have power under the Trustee Investments Act, 1961 to buy debentures and unsecured loan stocks for the 'narrower range' fund, the pressure on these stocks has become even greater.

The time to acquire them is on issue: at that stage they are free of stamp duty and the stockbroker's commission is less when they are in partly paid form. The investor, in considering a participation in an issue, will have regard to the nature of the company and the security offered. As regards the nature of the company, when times are good all companies are doing good business, so it is necessary to take a long-term look at the company's business, looking not only forward but backward also. Much money has been lost in secured debentures and a long tale of woe could be told. Investors should, therefore, keep to the staple industries and, in every case where an industry has been in real trouble in the past, should look for plenty of income cover before buying a debenture issued by a company in the group.

The security may be in the form of a fixed charge on specific assets or it may be solely a floating charge. The issue should be covered by assets by a minimum of twice and as regards income the cover should be at least two or three times (and more in certain cases) what is necessary to cover the annual service charge of the debenture. One must also consider the profits experience of the issuing company for the last five to ten years; a very erratic profits experience would militate against the success of the issue. Regard should also be paid to the term of the debenture. Investors ought to be wary if the term were long (or if there were no redemption date) and the effective rate of interest low. A selection of debenture stocks with varying coupons and maturity dates, showing the variation in yields as between the stocks is shown under Appendix 2.

In times when it is difficult to raise loan capital or equity shares on favourable terms a company will sometimes resort to the issue of *convertible loan stock*. The option given to convert into the company's ordinary shares on fixed dates at fixed prices is an attractive one. The investor will exercise the option only if it is in his favour, and if he takes no action he is still left with a secured debenture stock or an unsecured loan stock. Here are two examples of blue-chip convertible loan stocks. Both issues were very successful and the companies concerned got their money at a difficult time. In the former case the option quickly proved valuable, but in the latter the option dates passed without the option becoming attractive:

| *Stock* | *Issued at* | *Highest price* | *Value 27.7.73 of convertible loan stock if loanholder had converted £100 stock into shares at first opportunity* |
|---|---|---|---|
| I.C.I. 5¾% Convertible Loan Stock 1977–79 .. | 96 | 212 | 108 worth £257 |
| B.P. 6% Convertible Loan Stock 1976–80 .. .. | 99 | 115¼ | 48 worth £253 |

For the reasons indicated, few B.P. holders would have converted. The present price of the stock is 75 (27.7.73).

There is a differential in interest to distinguish between the investor's (or market's) assessment of the merits of each group of fixed-interest stocks *and* as between stocks in each group. It follows that *unsecured loan stocks* will have to offer a higher interest rate than a debenture of the same company. In certain circumstances – loan interest in arrear, etc. – the unsecured loan stockholder becomes entitled to a specific charge on the company's assets subject, of course, to the prior charges of any existing debentures, etc.

*Preference and Preferred Capital* (nominal value £1,279,540,000; market value £812,920,000). In the capital structure of a company this comes after the loan capital and before the ordinary and deferred share capital.

Preference shares rank before the ordinary shareholders on a winding-up. Further, not infrequently companies issue cumulative preference shares, in which case, if any dividend falls into arrear, the arrears have to be paid off before an ordinary dividend can be paid. Preference stocks and shares were at one time very popular – that is, before the cult of the ordinary share.

The preference share of a first-class company gives security of income and capital and until the advent of Corporation Tax it offered the investor a higher yield than that given on a prior loan stock. Now that preference share interest, unlike debenture and loan stock interest, is franked for Corporation Tax in the hands of an institutional investor and other investors liable to Corporation Tax, preference shares have acquired a special investment status – they have become popular as a means of acquiring high yielding franked income. Thus the demand for preference shares has put up their values and they now yield less than most unsecured loan stocks and debenture stocks. Perhaps I should mention that franked means that the company investor does not pay Corporation Tax on the income; thus a 5 per cent. preference share with a nominal value of £1 at a price of 50p gives a yield to a fund not liable to tax of 10 per cent. and to a fund liable to Corporation Tax a yield also of 10 per cent. net, whereas a debenture stock with a gross yield of 10 per cent. would be worth only £7·14 to a fund liable to Corporation Tax.

It follows that although preference shares are attractive to an investing company liable to Corporation Tax they represent an unattractive form of borrowing by a company that pays Corporation Tax. It works in this way: the interest on an unsecured loan stock or a convertible debenture or a mortgage debenture is a charge against the company's profits before paying Corporation Tax, whereas preference share interest is not allowable. It is because of the fact that preference share interest is paid out of profits which have suffered Corporation Tax that it is franked for Corporation Tax in the hands of investors liable to Corporation Tax. Because of the tax disadvantage to the company issuing the preference shares a number of preference share issues have been paid off by arrangement with the shareholders and I think while the tax position remains as at present, the repayment of preference shares will continue. Indeed, the nominal amount of quoted preference shares has dropped by over 25 per cent. since the onset of Corporation Tax.

Preference stocks are for the most part irredeemable. From the standpoint of inflation, they offer no protection to the investor but before the advent of Corporation Tax at times of high interest rates preference shares were attractive purchases and very much in favour.

Preference shares rank in security after debentures and unsecured loan stock but before the equity capital. Investors in the Dalton era who were tempted by irredeemable preference shares giving abnormally high rates of interest compared with that which was generally current at the time have had some nasty losses in preference shares.

Preference shares have sometimes to be issued at high rates of interest to attract investors. A new untried company at times of high interest rates had to offer particularly attractive yields – 9 per cent. and 10 per cent. have not been uncommon. Some of these companies have failed but others have been successful, having in the meantime attained blue-chip status. In the latter case the interest rates now look quite ridiculous, and at times of low interest rates the stocks have stood at very substantial premiums. Here are two preference shares, both with fantastic cover and one with a high coupon:

| *Share* | | *Price* | *Yield after allowing for expenses* | *Cover* |
|---|---|---|---|---|
| Shell 5½% 1st Cum. £1 Preference | .. | 54½p | £9·86% | 1,074 times |
| B.P. 8% 1st Cum. £1 Preference | .. | 75p | £10·42% | 59 times |

It is preferable to express cover in another way: suppose 5 per cent. of a company's available profits were needed for its debenture interest and 8 per cent. for its preference dividend, and it paid 50 per cent. in ordinary dividend, the priority percentages would be shown as follows:

| | | |
|---|---|---|
| Debenture interest | .. | 0– 5 |
| Preference interest | .. | 5– 13 |
| Ordinary dividend | .. | 13– 63 |
| Carry forward .. | .. | 63–100 |

There have been attempts to repay high-yielding preference shares by liquidating and reconstructing a company; in fact, in the House of Lords one of the law-lords expressed the opinion that it was the duty of a board of directors to repay a preference stock whenever this could be done to the benefit of the ordinary shareholders. Like many an *obiter dictum* by learned judges, this frightened for a while. Nothing much has happened since, and the various investors' protection societies would certainly put up some pretty effective resistance if boards tried to benefit equity holders at the expense of preference shareholders in this way.

For those charities, pension funds or individuals not subject to income tax at the full standard rate some preference shares, and some equities for that matter, had before the advent of Corporation Tax a particular disadvantage. I am referring to the shares of those companies which were then entitled to *double taxation relief* and thus recovered substantial tax suffered abroad in this way. Where the shareholder did not pay income tax or was liable at a reduced rate he could, prior to Corporation Tax, only recover what was termed the '*net U.K.*' rate, which was the amount of tax in the pound suffered in this country after allowing for double taxation relief. It will be noted that the higher the rate of recovery the lower the net U.K. rate. Indeed some companies, the oil companies for example, had net U.K. rates of nil. This kind of experience highlights the imponderables of investment. No investment manager can forestall tax changes which about-turn investment principles.

When in 1961 I wrote *Investments in Trust*, I mentioned that preference shares were out of favour but I believed their time would come again. Their time *has* come again, but for a reason which I had not anticipated.

As mentioned, some preference shares have fantastically high income cover. The Trustee Investments Act, 1961 gives all trustees power to buy preference shares but only for the 'wider range' fund where they compete with equities. Whilst the cult of the equity lasts I cannot see trustees buying preference shares unless the circumstances are very unusual.

The future of preference shares is somewhat obscured by the effect of the introduction of the imputation system of Corporation Tax which is dealt with further on page 99. Certainly the relative attractiveness of franked investment income in relation to unfranked income will be somewhat reduced. Assuming a company distributes all its profits in the form of dividends the old system, on the basis of a 40 per cent. Corporation Tax rate, would work out as follows:

*Example 1*

| | *Franked* | | *Unfranked* | |
|---|---|---|---|---|
| | £100 | | £100 | Income received |
| *less* | nil | | 40 | Corporation Tax |
| | 100 | | 60 | |
| Shareholders' gross dividend | £100 | Shareholders' gross dividend | £60 | |

i.e. franked income was more valuable to the company than unfranked income in the ratio of 100:60 or 1·67 to 1.

Under the new system (assuming, as is likely, a 50 per cent. Corporation Tax rate) the situation is:

*Example 2*

| | *Franked* | | *Unfranked* | |
|---|---|---|---|---|
| | £100 | | £100 | Income received |
| *less* | nil | | 50 | Corporation Tax |
| | 100 | | 50 | |
| | | | 50 | = Dividend |
| | | A.C.T.* | 21·4 | Offset against Corporation Tax |
| Shareholders' gross dividend | £100 | Shareholders' gross dividend | £71·4 | |

* A.C.T. is Advance Corporation Tax and represents tax of 30 per cent. after grossing up the net dividend.

i.e. franked income is more valuable than unfranked income in the ratio of 100:71·4 or 1·4 to 1. Although this might reduce the popularity of preference shares, this may be balanced by the fact that under the new system franked income if retained becomes more valuable in relation to unfranked income than under the old system.

Another interesting point with the new system of Corporation Tax is that the 1972 Finance Act stipulates that the dividend on all preference shares issued before 6th April, 1973, is to be reduced by 30 per cent.; thus the dividend on a 10 per cent. preference share now becomes 7 per cent. This is all very well if the rate of Advance Corporation Tax remains at 30 per cent., but if it falls in future years the gross income will fall, as although the net income will remain the same the tax credit will be less, and the non-taxpayer will recover less when he makes his repayment claim.

*Yield Differentials – Fixed-interest Stocks*

On the whole, supply and demand fixes fairly accurately the differentials in yield between the various groups of fixed-interest stocks. Here are some rough guides, assuming the stocks have similar coupons and similar redemption dates and assuming the yield on British government stocks to be *x* per cent. These are, as indicated, rough guides. I have known the differentials between British government stocks and good debentures almost to disappear, taking stamp duty into consideration:

| | |
|---|---|
| British government stocks .. .. .. | £*x*% |
| Home corporations .. .. .. .. | £*x* + 25p% |
| Public boards .. .. .. .. | £*x* + 37½p% |
| First-class dominion and colonial stocks .. | £*x* + 50p% |
| Good debentures .. .. .. .. | £*x* + 60p% |
| Good unsecured loan stocks .. .. | £*x* + 80p% |

Before the advent of Corporation Tax I expressed the view that a good preference share should attract a rate of interest of 62½p to 75p more than the yield on an irredeemable British government stock, but due to reasons already given the yield is somewhat less than that of a first-class debenture stock. Indeed, all I can state is that the yield on a good preference stock will depend upon the pressure of institutional investors who want to buy high-yielding franked income. My guess is that the yield on a good class preference share will remain somewhat below that of a first-class debenture stock. Certainly, any investor who is contemplating selling a preference share should hesitate if the true yield given up is more than what he could expect to get on a debenture stock, as a preference shareholder might, under existing conditions, be paid off on attractive terms.

*Switching Operations*

Obviously there will be times when comparative yields between the groups get out of step. Yields also get temporarily out of step within the groups themselves. This gives opportunities for switching, which is the happy hunting ground of the institutional investor. To take a simple example: an investor could, at a time when 3½ per cent. Conversion was relatively the cheaper stock after allowance for accrued interest, sell £2,000,000 3½ per cent. War Loan and invest the proceeds in 3½ per cent. Conversion and when the relative prices returned to normal sell the Conversion Loan and get back into War Loan – but of course to a larger amount. This type of switching helps to keep market prices in harmony and provides the larger investor with not insubstantial profits. The example I have given is switching in its most simple form. Switching itself is a most sophisticated art and I refer to it in greater detail in my book *Principles of Pension Fund Investment* (published by Hutchinson).

*Stamp Duty*

British government stocks are not subject to stamp duty; neither are certain corporation stocks, public board stocks and colonial government stocks. It is necessary to check whether a stock is or is not subject to stamp duty, as some stocks which would normally be liable have had the duty compounded for a single payment. An investor should certainly expect loan capital and preference stock to be subject to stamp and, as already indicated, he would endeavour to buy them when they were issued and in scrip form. Stamp duty is now 1 per cent. on the purchase of an investment. It was increased from ½ per cent. to 1 per cent. at the time of the First World War and from 1 per cent. to 2 per cent. on 1st August, 1947, and it reverted to 1 per cent. on 1st August, 1963.

CHAPTER 5

# Equities

*Introduction: The Case for Equities*

Ordinary shares which represent the equity of a company are the risk capital of industry. If we believe that in the long term Britain will expand her industries despite competition, stop-go and all the other difficulties; that we are still a virile nation; that in many things we shall continue to lead the world; if we believe in our great people, then we must believe in the growth of the equity of the component companies which make up British industry.

To any doubters I offer the profits and dividend figures of Marks & Spencer for the ten years to 1973.

PROFITS AND DIVIDENDS

| *Year ended 31st March* | *Turnover* £ | *Net profit before tax* £ | *Net profit after tax* £ | *Dividends* £ |
|---|---|---|---|---|
| 1964 | 201,494,000 | 25,070,000 | 12,220,000 | 8,503,000* |
| 1965 | 219,791,000 | 27,656,000 | 12,856,000 | 9,194,000* |
| 1966 | 238,015,000 | 29,818,000 | 18,468,000 | 16,793,000 |
| 1967 | 255,770,000 | 30,859,000 | 19,189,000 | 16,831,000 |
| 1968 | 282,306,000 | 33,871,000 | 20,121,000 | 17,370,000 |
| 1969 | 317,336,000 | 38,123,000 | 21,773,000 | 17,953,000 |
| 1970 | 360,935,000 | 43,705,000 | 24,955,000 | 20,197,000 |
| 1971 | 416,685,000 | 50,115,000 | 31,215,000 | 22,890,000 |
| 1972 | 463,022,000 | 53,766,000 | 34,416,000 | 25,246,000 |
| 1973 | 550,262,000 | 70,036,000 | 42,436,000 | 26,509,000 |

* Net; other years' gross.

Here are also the less dynamic profits and dividend figures of Decca Ltd for the ten years to 31st March, 1972:

| *Year ended 31st March* | *Turnover* £ | *Net profit before tax* £ | *Net profit after tax* £ | *Dividends* £ |
|---|---|---|---|---|
| 1963 | 28,000,000 | 2,968,147 | 1,449,533 | 689,000* |
| 1964 | 30,200,000 | 2,630,759 | 1,344,756 | 708,000* |
| 1965 | 36,900,000 | 3,939,143 | 2,067,648 | 801,000* |
| 1966 | 36,300,000 | 4,323,570 | 2,617,137 | 1,365,000 |
| 1967 | 40,000,000 | 4,466,083 | 2,525,585 | 1,436,000 |
| 1968 | 47,000,000 | 4,762,463 | 2,692,290 | 1,471,000 |
| 1969 | 48,500,000 | 3,070,841 | 1,529,614 | 1,445,000 |
| 1970 | 61,300,000 | 5,390,511 | 2,594,807 | 1,590,000 |
| 1971 | 66,700,000 | 3,092,296 | 1,569,677 | 1,406,000 |
| 1972 | 81,800,000 | 7,205,007 | 4,204,347 | 2,026,000 |

* Net; other years' gross.

There will be arguments as to who should benefit from our industrial expansion – capital, labour or the State, and in what proportions. At present all three benefit. In the reasonable (but capable of improvement) British capitalistic society in which we find ourselves, where we strive for 'fair shares for all', what is not taken by the State in taxation, or paid away in wages and salaries and other outgoings, belongs to the ordinary shareholder. And we can consider equity investment *only* against that background. We are forced to ignore the adverse effects of possible future political interference. The list of possible political risks reads like an investor's nightmare – threatened further nationalization, dividend limitation, government controls of materials, labour, and credit, the persecution of capital – and the greatest political risk of all, war.

In this matter of growth there are two elements – growth due solely to inflation and real growth. As to the former, here are some figures supplied by the *Economist* showing the consumer's price index for 1900 onwards:

| | | | |
|---|---|---|---|
| 1900 | 100 | 1960 | 511 |
| 1910 | 105 | 1961 | 525 |
| 1920 | 277 | 1962 | 547 |
| 1930 | 190 | 1963 | 558 |
| 1939 | 191 | 1964 | 576 |
| 1950 | 368 | 1965 | 605 |
| 1951 | 402 | 1966 | 627 |
| 1952 | 426 | 1967 | 641 |
| 1953 | 433 | 1968 | 670 |
| 1954 | 441 | 1969 | 706 |
| 1955 | 457 | 1970 | 744 |
| 1956 | 477 | 1971 | 801 |
| 1957 | 490 | 1972 | 856 |
| 1958 | 503 | 1973 | 942 (estimated) |
| 1959 | 507 | | |

The dividend that a shareholder receives might be two-and-a-half times what it was twenty years ago, but in real values it purchases no more; the shareholder has obviously only kept pace with inflation, although such a state of well-being would be the envy of a beneficiary under a fund which was limited to the investments stipulated under the Trustee Act, 1925, and which is still suffering from its effects despite the greater freedom now available under the Trustee Investments Act, 1961. An investor in equities would, however, expect to do better than merely to keep pace with inflation. The following graph shows that business turnover has more than kept pace with inflation since 1950:

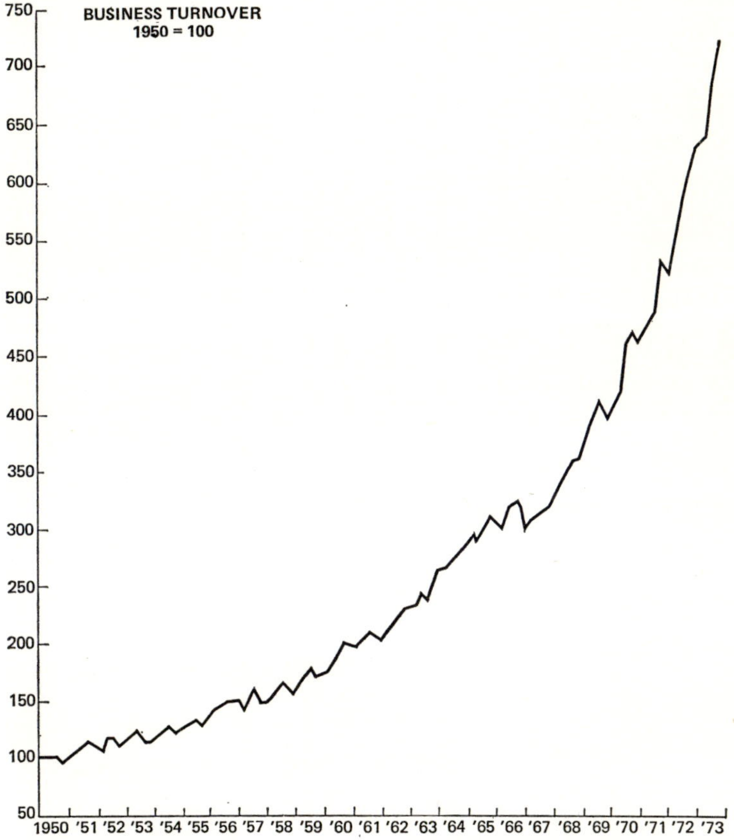


Based on the Midland Bank Index of Business Turnover (1950 = 100)

# Industrial Ordinary and Consols Yields Charted
## 1944–1966 (inclusive)

# Industrial Ordinary and Consols Yields Charted 1967–1973

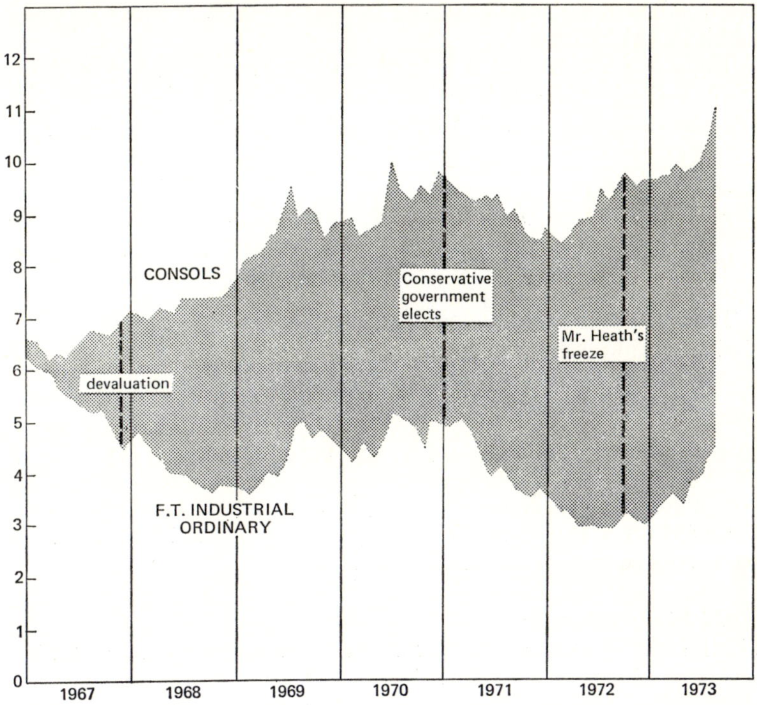


Let us now look at the performance of equity shares as compared with gilt-edged stocks. The graphs which appear on pages 18 and 19 show the comparative performance since 1924 of gilt-edged stocks and a selection of equities. It is to be noted, however, that over the selected period of nearly thirty years – quite a slice out of an adult's lifetime – it is only since 1952 that the growth in equity share values has become exciting. It will be further noted that in two periods, 1931–35 inclusive, and 1938–42 inclusive, and also in 1962 and 1966, gilt-edged stocks gave a superior performance. Indeed, the period 1910–45 inclusive was a difficult time for the equity investor. It included two world wars and perhaps the worst depression in history in the early thirties. When Wall Street crashed in October 1929, the

Dow Jones indices of common stocks dropped from a high of 381 to an eventual low of around 40 and the former figure of 381 was not equalled again until 1953. Certainly the period 1910–45 provided many a headache for the equity investor: we have short memories or historical blanks.

There is a saying that it is hard to beat the indices, but obviously many individual shares have beaten the index by a big margin. Here are two examples provided by a leading firm of stockbrokers:

| | | | *2.10.62* | *18.11 66* | *14.8.73* |
|---|---|---|---|---|---|
| Great Universal Stores | £100 invested in each in 1951 | Value | £3,066 | £3,150 | £5,468 |
| Legal and General | | | £1,638 | £860 | £1,959 |

In the early part of the century insurance shares showed outstanding growth and left the indices far behind.

There is another side to the picture. Here is a share which over a similar period has performed very differently, and I would stress that this was a more likely candidate for a purchase in 1951 than Great Universal Stores:

| | | | *2.10.62* | *18.11.66* | *14.8.73* |
|---|---|---|---|---|---|
| Babcock & Wilcox | £100 invested in 1951 | Value | £74 | £52 | £130 |

The graphs (pp. 38, 39) show the yield on consols as compared with the yield on a selection of ordinary shares for 1944 to date. The comparisons should be carefully noted.

*Yield Differentials*

Until 1959 it was axiomatic for the yield on the *Financial Times* selection of ordinary stock to give up to 2 per cent. more than consols as it was understood that risk capital should receive more yield by way of compensation.

The following highs and lows of these percentages rates will be of interest:

| | | *High* % | | *Low* % | |
|---|---|---|---|---|---|
| 2½% Consols | (i) | 11·42 | ( 9.8.73) | 2·53 | (13.9.47) |
| *F.T.* (Dividends) | (ii) | 7·14 | (27.2.57) | 3·05 | (15.8.71) |
| *F.T.* Earnings | (iii) | 18·14 | (27.2.58) | 4·40 | (19.9.68) |

(i) – from 1.1.1947
(ii) – from 19.4.1944
(iii) – from 6.12.1954

The high earnings yield at 27th February, 1958 makes one wonder how much the subsequent rise in equity values is due to a liberalization of dividend policy – quite a bit in my opinion.

Since 1959 investors have for the most part been prepared to accept a lower yield on equities because of the growth element in their dividends. Indeed in July 1961 consols had a yield of 2½ per cent. more than the dividend yield on the *Financial Times* Industrial Share Index compared with the more normal difference of 1 to 1½ per cent. more for Consols. Rather exceptionally in September 1962 the two yield paths recrossed for a few days. Since then the yield differential returned to the previous pattern of more for consols, but in October 1966, with equities right out of favour, the yields re-crossed again and it seemed that this pattern would persist for some months. However, after a month or two the yields reversed again and Consols now give the higher yield by a clear margin of over 7 per cent., which is exceptional and surely must in time narrow.

The yield difference between 2½ per cent. Consols and the yield on the *F.T.* Industrial Share Index (or the *F.T.* Actuaries All Share Index, as I prefer) is one of the indications as to the attractiveness of fixed-interest stocks or equities. When the yields draw closer it *could* be a signal for buying equities, and when 2½ per cent. Consols give a yield substantially more than the yield on the *F.T.* Industrial Share Index, it *might* be a signal for buying gilts. The differential cannot be relied upon entirely because if gilts were completely out of favour it might be the wrong time to buy them, certainly on the short term. Investment managers are all the time looking for some trigger mechanism to take them out of gilts into equities and vice versa. Quite a useful guide could be a graph of the ratio of the *F.T.* Actuaries Dividend yield to the yield of 2½ per cent. Consols.

One must enter a *caveat*. The thirty ordinary shares (see below) comprising the *Financial Times* Industrial Ordinary Share Indices include some high-yielding shares. The list is as follows:

Industrial shares comprised in the *Financial Times* Industrial Index.

Allied Breweries
Associated Cement
Beechams
Boots
Bow water Paper
British Leyland Corpn.
British Oxygen
Brown J
Cavenham
Courtaulds
Distillers
Dunlop Rubber
Electrical & Musical Inds.
General Electric
Glaxo
Grand Metropolitan Hotels
Guest Keen & Nettlefolds
Hawker Siddeley
Imperial Chemical
Imperial Group

| | |
|---|---|
| London Brick | Tate & Lyle |
| Marks & Spencer | Tube Investments |
| P. & O. Deferred | Turner & Newall |
| Plessey | United Drapery Stores |
| Spillers | Vickers |

At the time I wrote the first edition of this book I stated that the yield on a selection of top ranking blue-chip equities was in the region of 3 to 4 per cent., but that there were many well-known growth shares giving yields of under 2 per cent. Not all these low yields were justified by events and in the setback in equity share prices in the autumn of 1966 and the winter of 1966–67 low yielding equity shares suffered the biggest falls in value. This could hardly be unexpected with dividend limitation and a cutting back of the growth in profits. True yields on equities are considered in the chapter entitled 'Investment Analysis' (page 54).

In an address to the Industrial Society (then known as the Industrial Welfare Society) of 26th January, 1960, Mr Ross Goobey, F.I.A., F.S.S., F.I.S., a vigorous exponent of a 100 per cent. equity fund for pension funds, recalled that when he had addressed the Society in 1957 the *Economist Intelligence Unit* had just produced some staggering figures which showed the comparative results of investing £1,000,000 on 1st January, 1919, in equities and alternatively in 2½ per cent. Consols. With the gross income similarly reinvested at the end of each year, the equity fund by 1st January, 1957, would have amounted to £28,072,000, whereas the gilt-edged fund would have amounted to £3,696,000. He also stated that a study by a firm of stockbrokers showed that £1,000 invested on 1st January, 1913, in the under-mentioned companies would have amounted to £16,570 by 1st January, 1920, and £73,840 by 1st September, 1959:

| | *Value at 1st January, 1920* £ | *Value at 1st September, 1959* £ |
|---|---|---|
| Distillers Co. Ltd .. .. .. | 1,740 | 18,780 |
| J. & P. Coats Ltd .. .. .. | 960 | 720 |
| Guest Keen & Nettlefolds Ltd .. | 1,750 | 11,430 |
| Vickers Ltd .. .. .. | 940 | 1,840 |
| P. & O. Steam Navigation Co. .. | 1,950 | 4,010 |
| Courtaulds Ltd* .. .. .. | 9,230 | 37,060 |
| | £16,570 | £73,840 |

* Investment made on 1st September, 1913.

Equity share enthusiasts not unnaturally tend to choose the dates which produce the best results: certainly it has at times been good taking stock since 1954. To display the other side of the medal, an investment of a sum of money in 1928 in the equities comprising the indices quoted would have had to wait until 1946 before the value of the equities equalled their original total cost, despite inflation in the meantime. And if disinvested in 1932 or 1940, serious losses would have resulted.

I warned when this book was first published in March 1963 that we had had a Conservative government since October 1951 and although few would not expect that one day the pendulum would swing in a government more to the Left, the short-in-memory investor hardly ever thinks of statutory dividend limitation possibilities, really punitive taxation, further nationalization and the like. Since then we have had two Labour governments, and the *F.T.* Industrial Share Index has fallen from a high of 374·2 (16th June, 1966) to a low of 284·2 (8th November, 1966) and risen to a high of 521·9 on 19th September, 1969. At this time we have a Conservative government and an Index of around 425. In common parlance, 'What do you know?'

Ignoring the political aspect, one cannot stress too much the fact that there has been another industrial revolution since the Second World War, in fact, sparked off by it, and we must watch our relevancies if we compare today too rigidly with the first three decades of the century.

There is undoubtedly a strong case for investing trust funds in equities. The extent of the investment must depend upon the type of the fund; but more about this later. It is already apparent that investing in equities is not without its dangers. In settled equity markets the supply of shares is seldom adequate and prices are forced up. In boom times with too much money chasing too little stock, prices become unrealistic; prices can also be run up further in a fever of gambling; political factors can confuse; balance of payments can run against Britain; international relations become dangerous; confidence suffers a damaging setback. There is certainly scope for the display of a high standard of investment skill, knowledge and intuition.

CHAPTER 6

# Equity Groups and Diversification

HAVING settled in our minds that it is appropriate to invest in equities we have now to decide how to proceed.

*Equity Groups*

On 31st March, 1973, 3,341 equities were quoted on the London Stock Exchange and as mentioned previously these had a nominal value of £18,564,497,000 and a market value of £135,760,391,000. The grouping appears on page 5.

The *Financial Times* groups its selected list of 2,600 equities on its two penultimate pages as follows:

BANKS
BEERS, WINES, AND SPIRITS
BUILDING INDUSTRY, TIMBER, AND ROADS
CHEMICALS, PLASTICS, ETC.
CINEMAS, THEATRES, AND TV
DRAPERY AND STORES
ELECTRICAL AND RADIO
ENGINEERING AND METAL
FINANCE, LAND, ETC. (under TRUSTS, FINANCE, LAND)
FOOD, GROCERIES, ETC.
HIRE PURCHASE (immediately under BANKS)
HOTELS AND CATERERS
INDUSTRIALS (Miscellaneous)
INVESTMENT TRUSTS (under TRUSTS, FINANCE, LAND)
INSURANCE
MACHINE TOOLS
MOTOR AND AIRCRAFT TRADES
  Motors and Cycles
  Commercial Vehicles
  Components
  Garages and Distributors
NEWSPAPERS, PUBLISHERS
OILS
PAPER, PRINTING, ADVERTISING
PROPERTY
SHIPBUILDERS, REPAIRERS
SHIPPING
SHOES AND LEATHER
TEXTILES
TOBACCO
TRUSTS, FINANCE, LAND

In addition, the *Financial Times* quotes gold, tin, rubber, and tea shares under the various headings at the end of its price list.

*Diversification*

At first flush an equal amount invested in each of the 2,600 equities quoted in the *Financial Times* index would achieve complete diversification. But this would ignore the facts that:

(a) one or more groups may be going through a difficult trading experience and the time is not ripe to purchase a share in the group;

(b) some companies may not have a good history of growth – pedestrian, in fact – and are best left alone;

(c) some companies are in the giant class and others mere pigmies and we ought by comparison to invest, say, three times as much in the former as in the latter;

(d) some equities, although excellent, appear to be currently over-valued.

I favour diversifying a fund through the groupings of the *F.T.* Actuaries All Share Index. The advantages of this is that the index provides a ready means of testing the performance of your own fund.

Here are the component parts of that index showing the percentages of the groups and sub-groups to the whole.

It will not be sound investment policy to stick rigidly to these percentages as some groups or sub-groups may at times become unattractive temporarily for a variety of reasons. In the final column I give the limits within which one firm of stockbrokers operates when advising their own institutional clients.

EQUITY DISTRIBUTION (on market value)

| | *F.T.A. index* | *Proposed limits* |
|---|---|---|
| CAPITAL GOODS GROUP | | |
| Building Materials . . . . . . . . | 3·5 | 1·5– 5·5 |
| Contracting & Construction . . . . . . | 1·5 | 0– 3·5 |
| Electricals (excluding Electronics, Radio & TV) | 3·0 | 1·0– 5·0 |
| Engineering (Heavy) . . . . . . . . | 0·6 | 0– 2·6 |
| Engineering (General) . . . . . . . . | 4·5 | 2·5– 6·5 |
| Machine Tools . . . . . . . . . . | 0·3 | 0– 2·3 |
| Miscellaneous . . . . . . . . . . | 1·5 | 0– 3·5 |
| | 14·9 | |
| CONSUMER GOODS (DURABLES) GROUP | | |
| Electronics, Radio & TV . . . . . . . . | 2·4 | 0·4– 4·4 |
| Household Goods . . . . . . . . | 0·7 | 0– 2·7 |
| Motors & Distributors . . . . . . . . | 2·0 | 0– 4·0 |
| | 5·1 | |

| | *F.T.A. index* | *Proposed limits* |
|---|---|---|
| CONSUMER GOODS (NON-DURABLE) GROUP | | |
| Breweries | 3·4 | 1·4– 5·4 |
| Wines & Spirits | 1·5 | 0– 3·5 |
| Entertainment & Catering | 2·2 | 0·2– 4·2 |
| Food Manufacturing | 4·6 | 2·6– 6·6 |
| Food Retailing | 1·8 | 0– 3·8 |
| Newspapers & Publishing | 0·9 | 0– 2·9 |
| Packaging & Paper | 0·8 | 0– 2·8 |
| Stores | 8·3 | 6·3–10·3 |
| Textiles | 2·0 | 0– 4·0 |
| Tobacco | 2·1 | 0·1– 4·1 |
| Toys & Games | 0·1 | 0– 2·1 |
| | 27·7 | |
| OTHER GROUPS | | |
| Chemicals | 6·4 | 4·4– 8·4 |
| Office Equipment | 2·1 | 0·1– 4·1 |
| Shipping | 1·6 | 0– 3·6 |
| Miscellaneous (Unclassified) | 5·3 | 3·3– 7·3 |
| | 15·4 | |
| Oil | 9·6 | 7·6–11·6 |
| FINANCIAL GROUP | | |
| Banks | 6·0 | 4·0– 8·0 |
| Discount Houses | 0·3 | 0– 2·3 |
| Hire Purchase | 0·8 | 0– 2·8 |
| Insurance (Life) | 2·1 | 0·1– 4·1 |
| Insurance (Composite) | 3·8 | 1·8– 5·8 |
| Insurance (Brokers) | 0·7 | 0– 2·7 |
| Merchant Banks, Issuing Houses | 2·7 | 0·7– 4·7 |
| Property | 4·7 | 2·7– 6·7 |
| Miscellaneous | 0·6 | 0– 2·6 |
| | 21·7 | |
| Investment Trust Group | 5·6 | 3·6– 7·6 |
| TOTAL | 100% | |

I favour the stockbroker's pattern of distribution as a basis. The distribution percentages depend of course on the trading conditions of the industrial groups at the time of investment. Capital goods shares must be distinguished from consumer goods shares: the latter are generally far more dependable. Mere diversification is no substitute for sound judgement based on a careful appraisement of an investment.

Diversification and spread are to some extent interchangeable terms. By 'spread' I have in mind the limitation in value of the amount invested in any one equity. Remember that 'spread' does not imply a very large number of small holdings; the object is a participation in the broad groups of the country's industrial economy. It should be admitted at once that diversification on the lines suggested by the stockbroker is not possible with a small fund. In such a case we have either to rely on selecting the winners – those that have in the past beaten the indices and are likely in the future to do so again – those that look like up and coming index beaters (hardly suitable investments for the small fund) – or (and that I favour) to rely on one or more investment trust equities, or on unit trusts.

CHAPTER 7

# Helps to the Investor

THE investor has many sources to help him in making up his mind and to keep him in touch with the market and individual shares.

(1) The *Financial Times* is a mine of information and, *inter alia*, gives the following information:

(a) the daily list already referred to, of some 2,600 equities, with the mid-market price, current dividend, dividend yield, earnings cover, price/earnings ratio, and the highest and lowest prices for the current year;
(b) United Kingdom daily price indices for (i) British government securities, (ii) fixed-interest stocks, (iii) industrial ordinary, (iv) gold mines, (v) Consols yield per cent., (vi) equities earnings and dividend yield per cent., and (vii) number of dealings;
(c) *Financial Times* Actuaries Indices for the various groups and sub-groups (see below) including graphs for individual shares and how their performance compares with their sub-group's index;
(d) industry and other surveys (appearing on Mondays) and graphs of business statistics;
(e) Stock Exchange report and market summary;
(f) option rates and a list of the most active stocks;
(g) general investment news;
(h) dividend announcements and company reports and accounts;
(i) company meeting reports;
(j) Wall Street prices, the Dow Jones, Standard and Poor's indices, and various other international indices;
(k) new issue news;
(l) money market report;
(m) a selection of provincial, commonwealth, and continental stock exchange quotations; and
(n) base metal and commodity price changes;

(o) prognostications of economists.

(2) *F.T. Actuaries Stock and Share Indices.* This is another valuable service rendered by the *Financial Times.*

The indices cover 500 grouped industrial shares referred to as the '500 Share Index' and 651 shares referred to as the 'All Share Index' which additionally includes a financial group, consisting of banks, discount houses, hire purchase, insurance (life), insurance (composite), insurance brokers, merchant banks, issuing houses, property shares, and a separate group, investment trusts.

There are also separate indices for rubber, tea, copper, mining finance and tin shares.

As regards fixed-interest stocks there are indices for (a) 20-year government stocks, (b) 20-year redeemable debentures and loans, (c) investment trust preference, and (d) commercial and industrial preference shares.

The All Share Index of 651 shares is grouped as follows: *Capital Goods* (184 stocks), Building Materials (29), Contracting and Construction (22), Electricals (excl. Light Electronics) (16), Engineering (Heavy) (15), Engineering (General) (64), Machine and Other Tools (14), Miscellaneous (24). *Consumer Goods* (*Durable*) (60), Light Electronics, Radio, TV (14), Household Goods (16), Motors and Distributors (30). *Consumer Goods* (*Non-Durable*) (170), Breweries (16), Wines and Spirits (8), Entertainment, Catering (16), Food Manufacturing (24), Food Retailing (18), Newspapers, Publishing (16), Packaging and Paper (15), Stores (28), Textiles (20), Tobacco (3), Toys and Games (6). *Other Groups* (86), Chemicals (22), Office Equipment (10), Shipping (10), Miscellaneous (41), Oil (3).

These make up the 500-Share Index: Financial (101), Banks (6), Discount Houses (8), Hire Purchase (5), Insurance (Life) (9), Insurance (Composite) (8), Insurance (Brokers) (8), Merchant Banks (18), Property (29), Miscellaneous (10), Investment Trust Group (50).

(3) *The weekly investment journals, Investors' Chronicle and Stock Exchange Gazette, Economist, Investors' Review, Investors' Guardian* etc., are also a great help, as are the City pages of the daily and Sunday newspapers.

(4) *The Exchange Telegraph* and the *Moodie Service* are invaluable. The professional investor tends to take these two services for granted. Both provide a truly wonderful service; almost all known and relevant information concerning a company appears on the cards and information sheets.

I would especially like to draw attention to the two Moodie books entitled *Industrial Trustee Companies*, Part 1 covering industrial trustee companies, and Part 2 banks, hire purchase, insurance, investment trusts, mining, finance, property, smaller industrials and overseas companies. Together they cover a total of nearly 950 shares with charts of performance and other very valuable information. These books are published quarterly, the service at present costs £18·50 per annum. There is a 'pocket' edition for the small investor priced at £2·75.

(5) There has already been a reference to *indices and graphs*. These are most useful in indicating trends, and many theories are based on graphs and charts. In addition to the *Financial Times* Equity Index, indices are provided by the Institute of Actuaries, *The Times*, and Moodie's Services.

(6) *Charts*. There are those who are great believers in charts. Charts are based on the theory that the market is always right and that by charting the prices over a period the resultant chart will tell the chartist whether it is a time to sell or buy the share and enable him generally to make some prognostications as to its future performance.

I believe that charts can be helpful but I find the language of the chartist off-putting. Here is a quotation: 'Well, the most recent prices seem to have broken through a resistance level on the down side, indicating a bearish trend, which is further evidenced by a market price gap on the right-hand dip of the shoulder formation.'

(7) *Stockbrokers*. The wise investor, whether an individual or a corporation, should work in close collaboration with a stockbroker. Some of the larger firms of stockbrokers provide an excellent statistical service and pride themselves on the probing power of their investment analysis processes and methods. Later I will refer again to stockbrokers and mention the kind of information they must be given if their help is to be sought effectively for the varying types of trust and investors. The average stockbroker is a serious, conscientious, competent, and reasonable practitioner of the art of investment. Give him full information and state the problem clearly. The Institutional investor will normally deal with a number of stockbrokers.

Most stockbrokers have their pet investments: it is not possible for one firm to specialize in the whole list of quoted investments. One leading firm of stockbrokers well known to me closely follows about 150 industrial companies, applying investment analysis principles to them, keeping records of their earnings and dividends over the past ten years, capital employed, rate of profit on capital, and twice a year issuing a most useful book of information concerning these companies. In addition, this firm watches another 70 equity second-liners, as they call them.

The professional investor will never follow blindly the advice of a stockbroker or any other investment authority; he takes the responsibility – the stockbroker merely advises. The trustee must therefore be prepared to exercise his judgement and stand by it. The work of stockbrokers in the field of investment analysis and research is referred to in the chapter headed 'Investment Analysis'.

(8) *Investment protection societies,* in looking after the interests of their own members, also protect other shareholders. The two important groups are the Insurance Protection Committee of the British Insurance Association and the Investment Committee of the Investment Trusts Association. The National Association of Pension Funds and the Association of Unit Trust Managers also have an investment protection committee.

(9) *The Annual Reports and Accounts of Companies,* and the speeches of their chairmen, are useful guides to the investor. These do not disclose all that many would desire to know. Obviously a company is not going to give away its secrets, neither will it wish to give information to its competitors. Investors should endeavour to 'get to know' the chairman of a company. Some are over-optimistic – some very cautious – and in reading a chairman's statement, it is good to 'know' him. Since the enactment of the Companies Act, 1948, companies with subsidiaries have had to publish consolidated accounts. This has been of inestimable help to investors and investment analysts. There is a thirst among professional investors for fuller information, and this was apparent from evidence given to the Jenkins Committee, prior to the 1967 Companies Act. Many were disappointed that this Act lagged behind the recommendations of the Committee, but a new Act (the Bill has recently been published) will it is hoped go considerably further by the time it becomes law than its predecessor. Among other things it proposes: (1) to make 'insider trading' in a company's shares an indictable offence – 'insider trading' is dealing actively in a company's shares by directors and others who have inside knowledge of the company's affairs; (2) that full details must be disclosed in the company's report and accounts of the holdings of shares in other companies in excess of 10 per cent. whether held beneficially or as trustees or in other ways (the City

term for building up such blocks of shares is Warehousing); (3) that details of the director's service agreements and dealings in the company's shares must be disclosed; (4) that details of the company's material acquisitions, realizations and contracts must be disclosed.

(10) *Market reviews.* A number of firms of stockbrokers give monthly reports on the economic situation with information on individual industries. In at least one case the economic review is written by a well-known economist. In addition, one leading firm details under group headings the equities the firm especially follows, with current buying price, yield *after expenses* (why is this not common practice?), twelve-month price range, with a figure showing *the ratio* of the average dividend yield on the equity since the last final dividend to the *Financial Times* average yield over the same period, and similarly the current ratio. The ratio shows at once the market's assessment of the share – under 100 means better than average; over 100 means inferior to average. The ratio might point to a share being over-valued or under-valued. It is just one of the factors in a welter of factors to bear in mind.

(11) *Statistics.* Statistics abound and the investor is bombarded with them – trade figures, gold reserves, employment figures, production figures, comparative trading, articles by leader-writers – all blast the investor with science. Much of it, however, arrives late. It is still possible for a large company which hitherto has had almost uninterrupted success suddenly and absolutely unexpectedly to report a loss on the year's trading or a dramatic fall in profits. Shades of the, at the time much recommended, Rolls Razor and the Associated Fire Alarm shares. Similarly, substantially increased profits are disclosed unexpectedly. Ponder too on the unexpected Rolls Royce debacle. To guard against the former and to take advantage of the latter is the aim of the professional investment adviser. He watches the figures of each industry as a whole, whether orders are going up or down, the changes in the labour force, and winkles out information on profit margins, wage claims, etc., etc. Some even visit the company's works and interview the managing director.

The professional economist, whom I find generally to be an incorrigible pessimist, utters his prognostications. The trouble often is that the cyclone, which the statistics predict will soon hit us, has already blown itself out in the form of a modest storm and in reality we are about to experience a period of good trading weather; but owing to the delay in supplying figures there is not even an identifying patch of blue sky as big as a pocket handkerchief on the distant economic horizon.

International figures and statistics are even less dependable – they are still further behind; they are prepared on a variety of different bases and, being often dressed up to suit home consumption, they sometimes give a false picture. One economist, the late Lady Rhys Williams, once told me that what was wanted was an 'economic time clock', wound up and regulated by information secured by the United Nations who would have power to dig out the relevant information from the nations concerned. It is a further refinement of, 'Spot that coming depression now and disperse it'. Incidentally, I wonder sometimes whether governments have not got depression and recession neuroses and I ask myself the question, 'Was that squeeze really necessary?'

CHAPTER 8

# Investment Analysis and Other Methods of Selection

*Introduction*

I am proposing to make an exception in this chapter by repeating it exactly as it appeared in the first edition, not, as everywhere else, to bring the text and the figures up to date, and at the end of the chapter to make a few comments.

My reasons for this are:

(1) The chapter, which was written towards the end of 1962, is of some historic interest; indeed at the time it gathered much press comment, mainly favourable.

(2) Although yields at the time on both equities (particularly equities) and fixed interest were appreciably lower the yields are comparable; they are historic and quite suitable for illustration purposes.

(3) By repeating the text I reveal both the strength and weaknesses of investment analysis and under comment I show to some extent how investment analysis has progressed since the chapter was written.

(4) I demonstrate the human limitations of forecasting the future, even if it is based on intelligent and reasoned estimates and thinking, as distinct from crystal ball gazing.

*Author's Views Expressed in the First Edition (1963)*

I now repeat the text of the chapter in full; my comments appear on page 59.

Even the wildest enthusiast would not describe security analysis as an exact science, but it does endeavour to use scientific measurements for the assessment of equities. It is a post-war development in England which has its origins in the United States of America. Those engaged upon security analysis are devoted to it, and I have witnessed real progress during recent years. Further progress will take place, especially as and when industrial companies publish more data. Obviously security analysis can take no account of political threats – it is for others to assess these investment-wise. The security analyst is dealing with industrial facts and figures. He examines the past and from his findings endeavours to predict the future.

As a full security analysis is a long job, taking several weeks when it is first done, a firm of stockbrokers with a team of analysts will concentrate on a limited number of companies. A fair-sized team will be needed to produce as many as seventy-five full analyses and to maintain them up to date as fresh accounts come out. The team will endeavour to cover a ten-year period. For their data they will rely upon the respective companies' reports and accounts, periodic turnover and profits statements, chairmen's speeches, the figures of production such as the Trade and Navigation accounts, *Board of Trade Journal*, the selling literature and house journals of the companies involved and any appropriate references in the daily and weekly financial journals – in fact, a library service. It needs no imagination to realize that, in the case of a large company with diverse interests and many associated companies, research of this nature is a big undertaking. This research is aimed at producing for the ten-year period the following information *inter alia*:

(1) Capital structure, with a note of the gearing.
(2) Growth in assets year by year, with percentages.
(3) Sales – home and overseas (if appropriate).
(4) The geographical distribution of the company's business expressed as percentages.
(5) Information concerning the company's research programme: this is all part of assessing the drive behind the business.
(6) Assessment of the management; not an easy matter, but none of these things is easy, though the exercise in total is rewarding.
(7) Ascertainment, from a study of the figures for sales over the ten years (or a lesser period if ten years' figures are not available), the percentage annual increase in sales.
(8) Calculation of the trading profit over the years as a percentage of sales, also the percentage rate earned over the years on the company's assets.
(9) Calculation of the dividend pay-out rate (i.e. percentage of profits paid out in dividend).

Not all these are readily available and in particular only a very small proportion of companies give turnover figures. This is by far the most important omission from company statistics, and the security analysts hope that the Jenkins Committee's recommendations on this point will be acceded to.

When the record of the past ten years has been ascertained, the next task is that of estimating future profits. The analyst usually tries to do this from the angle of both sales and profit margins and to check the results by earnings on total capital employed, so the absence of figures for sales is a real deprivation. It is not usually considered worthwhile to estimate profits for a longer period than five years ahead and, even for such a period, the estimates can be no more than a guide, although they are much more valuable than the hopeful and unsupported estimates of pre-security-analysis days: here I quote an investment analyst. On the other hand, short-term estimates of earnings and dividends for the current year are generally fairly near the mark.

It will be seen that, with the trends of the last ten years established, it will be possible to make estimates for the ensuing year and for the next five years as follows:

(a) future sales;
(b) profit on sales, less the appropriate debits;
(c) available for ordinary shares;
(d) per cent. earned on ordinary shares;
(e) dividend.

From all the foregoing data an estimate of earnings and dividends for the next five years is made, and finally the analyst endeavours to estimate the value of the shares. To do this he may calculate for the past ten-year period the mean dividend yield each year in respect of the company analysed, after making all the adjustments for rights and scrip issues, etc.: he could use the earnings yield instead if he so wished. The result is then compared over the same years with the mean yield on the investments making up the *Financial Times* Industrial Index or any other index which might be chosen. This will immediately show whether the company has a market rating higher than the companies comprising the index.

Let us assume that the ratio of the company's dividend yield to the *Financial Times* yield is 70 per cent. Taking the *Financial Times* index dividend yield as 5 per cent. the share could be capitalized on a basis of 3·5 per cent. With an estimated dividend of 37½ per cent., at the end of the five-year period a 5s. share would then be worth 53s. 6d. If the current price of the share is 42s. 9d. based on a current dividend of 27 per cent. with a current yield of £3 1s. 3d. per cent. and in five years' time the share *is* worth 53s. 6d., this is in theory equivalent to buying at approximately £80 a stock which is redeemable at par at the end of five years.

To give another example and to put it another way; suppose on a security analysis it was estimated that the dividends of the company analysed would rise by 10 per cent. per annum over the next five years and 3 per cent. per annum thereafter, a share standing on the current yield basis of £3 3s. 3d. would, if the dividend were so raised, give a growth yield analogous to a redemption yield of 7 per cent. gross. By way of comparison, 2½ per cent. Savings Bonds 1964-67, current price 92¾, redeemable at par in just under five years, give a current yield of £2 13s. 10d. gross and a redemption yield of £4 5s. 0d. gross. The exercise is in the realm of mathematics and is a little difficult for the non-mathematician to comprehend. I gather from a leading firm of brokers that security analysis development is proceeding on the lines indicated, for, I am informed, it would appear to be the only means of convincing hard-headed institutional and other professional investors that they should consider buying equities at their current yields rather than take the 5 per cent. to 6½ per cent. currently available from fixed-interest stocks.

To take this new development a stage further the security analysts estimate the annual growth in dividend for a number of companies. Although some companies are given a ten-year initial growth, generally a five-year growth is assumed with a tailing-off growth of 3 per cent. p.a. thereafter. With these data, true growth yields to a purchaser are calculated. I feel that a consideration of growth yield is a real advance in investment thought. Here are some figures obtained from the tables prepared by the stockbrokers showing what annual growth is required for five or ten years to give a true yield of 7 per cent.:

| *Yield on purchase price* % | *Five years** % p.a. | *Ten years** % |
|---|---|---|
| 0·97 | 50 | 23 |
| 1·95 | 23 | 13 |
| 2·58 | 16 | 9 |
| 3·04 | 11 | 7 |
| 3·48 | 7 | 5 |
| 4·00 | 3 | 3 |

* 3 per cent. p.a. thereafter.

By taking the current yield of a share and inspecting the tables, the rate of growth required to give a growth yield of, say, 7 per cent. can be ascertained. During the past year, for example, there have been some property companies and some life assurance companies on current yields of 17s. per cent. to £1 5s. per cent. Assuming initial growth yields for ten years, with 3 per cent. p.a. thereafter, the annual growth in dividends for ten years would have to be of the order of 25 per cent. and nearly 17 per cent. per annum respectively to give growth yields of 7 per cent.

This firm keeps a table with forecasts of dividend growth rates for nearly forty companies. Here are a few examples:

| *Equity* | *Gross current yield* | *Forecast growth five years dividend growth rate* | *Gross growth yield* |
|---|---|---|---|
| British Motor .. .. | 6·90 | 10·7 | 11·8 |
| United Steel .. .. .. | 6·40 | 10·7 | 11·2 |
| Imperial Chemical .. .. | 5·24 | 7·0 | 9·0 |
| Woolworths .. .. .. | 4·12 | 7·5 | 7·8 |
| Dunlop .. .. .. | 4·19 | 6·1 | 7·7 |
| Unilever .. .. .. | 3·53 | 10·7 | 7·6 |
| Metal Box .. .. .. | 3·44 | 9·9 | 7·4 |
| Beechams .. .. .. | 3·81 | 5·7 | 7·2 |
| Marks & Spencer .. .. | 3·12 | 10·7 | 7·1 |
| Boots .. .. .. .. | 2·67 | 9·3 | 6·3 |
| Jaguar Cars .. .. .. | 1·38 | 22·4 | 5·7 |

In view of past records the last three shares, at least, could be given initial growth rates for ten years. In which case the growth yields would be as follows:

| | |
|---|---|
| Marks & Spencer | 8·3 |
| Boots | 7·2 |
| Jaguar Cars | 8·1 |

One firm of stockbrokers keeps a record of some 600 equities and calculates for each share the ratio of (a) the price, (b) the dividend yield, (c) the earnings yield to those of an industrial share index comprising 500 shares. The figures are recorded weekly and the stockbrokers claim they enable them to measure the past performance of the share against the performance of shares generally. It is claimed that these plottings highlight when a share is historically dear or cheap, at least on its past record, or whether it is performing unusually in any way. A steady falling of ratings before the declaration of dividend might imply some intelligent selling. Interesting situations develop when the ratios do not all move in the same direction.

Another firm of stockbrokers analyses under the various industries the accounts and balance sheets of over 400 companies. The figures grouped under industries are kept in booklet form. This serious piece of research is directed towards assessing the effectiveness or otherwise of management. A comparative analysis is made of the growth in (a) earnings, (b) assets, (c) total capital employed, (d) in the value of plant and premises; cash flow which is depreciation charged plus profits retained is worked out, as is also the percentage profit on assets. It must be stressed that the figures, which relate to a period which has passed, by up to nine months, must be considered against the current experience of the industry. But if the prospects of the industry are good then the data available enable one to choose the share of the dynamic company.

The crucial question is: 'Will the next five years show, in respect of the companies analysed, a similar growth to that of the last ten years?' If not, the security analysts and others may have predicted optimistically, but what they have done, and are doing, is an invaluable work in applied investment skill. The exercise itself teaches much.

## Investment Analysis

*Author's Comments (1973)*

1. Since November 1962 there has been a further liberalization in the information given by companies and available to analysts. This has been helped by the Stock Exchange which as from 1st September, 1966 requires a company to furnish to the Stock Exchange *inter alia* the following information before a new quotation will be given, or a further issue of capital is approved for dealings:

(a) To notify, without delay, changes in directors or in the nature of the business.
(b) To provide half-yearly interim reports.
(c) To include in the accounts of the company many of the proposals embodied in the 1967 Companies Act (see below).
(d) To accept designated accounts – shades of the diehard Registrar – and the end of a somewhat autocratic rule.

The 1967 Companies Act, although a disappointment to both chartered secretaries and to investment analysts as it lags behind the

Jenkins Committee recommendations, requires a company *inter alia*:

(i) to improve its Report and Accounts so as to give more information to shareholders, to break down the turnover to show which of its activities really produce the profits, to show the value of exports and in fact to add any matters material for the appreciation of the state of the company's affairs by its members,
(ii) to show how much the board and highly paid executives of the company are earning,
(iii) to disclose more information about its own subsidiary companies and about its investments in other companies where these are sizeable,
(iv) to keep a register of directors,
(v) to keep a file of directors' service contracts for inspection,
(vi) to set up a register for the large blocks of the company's shares, showing who are in fact the beneficial owners of the shares. This should prevent other companies building up sizeable shareholdings as the first step along the road to a takeover.

This additional information aids investment analysis, but may involve analysts in taking longer and longer to come to their final conclusions. The market-man will interpret the information immediately in price movements, but he is concerned with very short-term reaction whereas the analyst is concerned with the longer term.

2. Not all of the estimated growth rates which are given on page 58 materialized over the period 1962 to 1966 and for the autumn and winter 1966–67 growth was a minus quantity. However, since 1967 the rate of growth in company profits has accelerated appreciably and over the year to August 1973 rose 21 per cent. These recent years have come to the rescue, and the average growth in profits over the last ten-year period was 6·3 per cent.

Misery me, the trials of the forecaster. In the partnership of art and science in investment there is no sign yet of science becoming the senior partner.

3. Following up (2), I mentioned on page 58 that during 1962 some property companies and some life assurance companies had current yields of between 17s. and £1 5s. 0d. per cent. The comparative yields in 1966–67 tell a very different story. The *F.T.* Actuaries–Property Group had a dividend yield of $5\frac{1}{4}$ per cent. (some of the

best-known property companies offered yields of 6 per cent.), just covered by earnings, while the *F.T.A.* Life Assurance Group yielded $4\frac{1}{4}$ per cent. As there has been very little in the way of dividend increases between 1962 and 1966 the increases in yield mean depreciation in the share price over the period of the order of 60 per cent.; all due to very exceptional circumstances, but it does demonstrate the dangers of putting all your investment eggs in two group baskets.

4. Messrs Phillips & Drew who pioneered growth yields in this country are now feeding into their computer investment analysis data together with various estimates including that of growth with a view to estimating the relatively cheapest shares. The aim is the selection of equities by computer. The method is proving reasonably successful so far but of the ten factors fed into the computer four are estimates and obviously the answer the computer gives depends largely on these estimates. Nevertheless I regard this as another useful weapon in the investment manager's armoury.

Messrs Hoare & Co., the firm referred to on page 58 as keeping various details of 600 equities, has now extended the list to 1,000 industrial companies plus 200 others in the financial group. The companies are subdivided under nearly ninety industrial group headings, and comprehensive statistical data are provided from a base date of 1st January, 1965.

This firm publish weekly market data on all these companies and with the aid of their computer calculate income account and balance sheet items as a percentage of the ordinary share capitalization; also indices of dividend and earnings yield ratios and indices of share price and asset value relative to the industrial sub-group and to all industry (the 1,000 companies mentioned above). Statistics are also presented in chart form for the share price and the dividend and earnings movement since 1st January, 1965 for the individual companies, together with charts for the price and dividend yield relative to all industry (1,000 companies) – again with a base date of 1st January, 1965.

5. Then there is Denis Weaver's book, *Investment Analysis* (Longmans, 1971), which the layman would find rather technical. Mr Weaver, who is an actuary and a pioneer of investment analysis in Britain, is a doughty advocate of it, as are many before him, in the United States.

6. It is not surprising in view of what has been written under the heading of comment that investment analysis has some vigorous critics, too. Mr Ian Little had a swipe at investment analysis in his

celebrated paper 'Higgledy Piggledy Growth'. Dr J. T. Ross Jackson in the *New Scientist* wrote: 'Many theories, facile and sophisticated, have been put forward to aid prediction of the price of stocks and shares. They crumble when statistical analysis reveals that price variations conform very closely to something as simple as the flip of a coin.' Carl Borch was even more devastating when he wrote: 'With the present state of our knowledge it seems quite fair to consider analysts, at least those who belong to the technical school, as the astrologers of our century. The horoscopes they prepare for individual stocks are based on price behaviour in the past, but they equally may be based on the constellation of the stars when the companies were formed. . . . Security Analysts are respected members of our society, like astrologers once were, they are amply rewarded when their predictions prove right – as they are bound to be in about half the cases.'

Notwithstanding, I am sure investment analysis has come to stay and will, I predict, become an ever greater force in investment; and its greatest ally will be the computer.

## CHAPTER 9

# Choosing Equities

WELL, it is against the background of these things of shreds and patches mentioned in the last two chapters that the professional investor conjures up his investment selection. Much of it is trial and error, but it is all a genuine effort to convert the art of investment into a science. I admire greatly these 'back-room boys' who are striving for perfectionist investment. Nevertheless I have known successful investors who seem to be able to manage with only a modicum of science and to make quick and correct decisions more by flair and instinct – they are probably helped by a good memory and native shrewdness. And do not forget that the human computer, the brain, is a great store-house of information, and that many a right judgement is based on forgotten information stored there. I have known others, completely saturated with science, who always seem to have a reason for doing nothing until the market trend is more or less observable to all. Perhaps it is a case, to quote a sage, of 'too much thought inhibiting action!'

Choosing equities is a routine matter for someone who has been choosing them for years. He will already have established in his mind a panel of equity shares, a selection based on years of experience and knowledge. He will know what shares are in, what shares are out. As to the rest, some will be borderline and others he may not yet have considered. Even to an expert this is understandable – there are well over 3,000 equity shares quoted on the London Stock Exchange.

In choosing equities I find it is helpful to have the list of possible shares presented under the following headings:

| *Name* | *Price* | *Dividend* | *Yield %* | *Dividend and earning % for last two years* | *Highest and lowest price for the year* | *P./E. ratio* |
|---|---|---|---|---|---|---|

If the list exclusively contained shares which were on my panel, the only consideration necessary would be whether they were suitable to the particular fund and, if so, whether the price was right. On the other hand, if the list included shares with which I was unfamiliar or as to which I had reservations, I would consult the Moodies sheet and/or the Exchange Telegraph card and would consider *inter alia* the following information concerning the company:

(a) business transacted by the company and its subsidiaries;
(b) the list of directors;
(c) amount of capital and capital structure of the company;
(d) yield on capital invested;
(e) earnings trend over the last ten years;
(f) dividend record over the last ten years;
(g) details of scrip and rights issued; and
(h) current prospects as perhaps revealed in the chairman's statement.

To sum up: has the company shown real growth and is the growth likely to continue?

*Considerations in Choosing Shares*

In selecting equity shares regard must be had to the special circumstances of the investor, such as the tax position and the size of the fund: this is dealt with more fully later.

The following points should be borne in mind:

(1) The company should be of reasonable size – the Trustee Investments Act, for example, mentions paid-up capital of £1,000,000.
(2) The company's business must, so far as is possible, be a stable one, and the industry an expanding one.
(3) The earnings must show a steady growth trend. Companies with long and exceptionally favourable records of earnings usually prove to be the best investments.
(4) The management must be good; this can be judged on past results and market opinion.
(5) The earnings' cover for the dividend must be adequate. Under the original Corporation Tax system it was generally agreed that the earnings' cover for the dividend should not be less than 1·75 times although there were always some blue-chip exceptions to this rule including, of course, investment trusts.

Under the new system, which operated from 6th April, 1973, the total amount of Corporation Tax paid by a company depends on the proportion of profits distributed; thus dividend cover becomes rather difficult to define.

Under the old system it was easy to calculate the price/earnings ratio – the earnings per share divided into the share price. But the calculation becomes complicated under the new system. There have been at least three definitions of earnings proposed – all with their supporters – which lead to different figures for the price/earnings ratio. However, no doubt a standard measure will emerge in the end – although it may not necessarily take the form of a price/earnings ratio.

(6) The dividend yield must be 'right' for the share, and this is in the main a matter of investment judgement. Some hold the view that the true yield on an equity can be calculated only in retrospect. Others, helped by security analysis, endeavour to project the yield for the next five years in an effort to estimate what future dividend increases are likely to be made. The present price may assume too much, in which case the shares are too dear.

(7) Where possible, enter the market through rights issues; except when a boom is in full blast the mere mention of a rights issue, unless it is a very modest one, depresses the price of a share. Then again, the price of rights tends to be depressed by selling on the part of those shareholders who are unable to take up their rights in whole or part. Another favourable factor is that rights are not subject to stamp duty, and the stockbroker's commission is less when rights are nil paid or partly paid.

(8) Some investors consider the price value of the shares against the net balance sheet assets. A share with a poor dividend record becomes especially interesting from takeover prospects if on an assets basis the shares are under-valued or if the company has a high proportion of cash assets. With the exception of investment trusts and property companies, shares are normally valued on an earnings and dividend basis – in fact, I could name some very successful companies with little in the way of assets whose shares give a very low yield. It therefore follows that some unexciting shares do become under-valued on an assets basis, but do not assume that they necessarily have takeover prospects.

(9) There are fashions in shares, and popular support can

over-price a good share so far as the professional investor is concerned.

(10) Alternatively, a share may become unpopular temporarily, the company's difficulties being over-emphasized. This gives opportunities for acquiring the shares cheaply in the belief that good management will successfully overcome present difficulties.

(11) Avoid the shares of countries which are unfavourable to the investor.

(12) In general, avoid a share that has not a free market.

(13) The prices of individual shares ebb and flow according to general market conditions, and there is scope for intelligent buying.

(14) The shares of any company which has had one very bad set-back should be treated with great caution when it appears to have recovered. History often repeats itself with companies.

(15) Finally there is no precise mathematical way of assessing whether a share is cheap – there are so many imponderables. In the end the decision is a matter of judgement. One stock-broker friend of mine keeps a crystal ball on his desk symbolizing the fact that often there can be no known correct answer to an investment problem.

*Panel of Shares*

Some investors advocate having a panel of shares, and this is what in fact the stockbrokers, referred to earlier, are aiming at. One hundred and fifty equities, if they are rightly chosen, are sufficient as a selection ground for most portfolios. I feel that increasing the number of shares under consideration to an unmanageable number is no way of diversifying. You may not do better by spreading your allocation to the chemical industry over all the chemical shares quoted on the Stock Exchange as compared with putting the lot in I.C.I. I will go further; you will almost certainly do worse and give yourself greatly increased work. Provided the panel is not a fixed thing it has its virtues; the components of the panel will have to stand up from time to time to vigorous tests, and if any fail the test the shares will have to be dropped from the panel and replaced by others which in the meantime have become worthy of panel status.

*Investing Abroad*

When conditions in Britain are stable and industry is allowed reasonable freedom from political interference there is much to be said for concentrating on British investments: keeping in touch with British equities is a big enough task for anyone. Nevertheless, there is a case for having an interest in overseas equities, and one way of achieving this is to buy investment trust equities whose portfolios have a substantial participation in North America. In this way the investor transfers all the headaches which go with overseas investments – political risks, currency risks, taxation position, problems of supervision – to the investment trust managers. As an alternative to the investment trust, there are unit trusts which operate in most of the large countries of the world under competent management and where the security aspect is sound.

A further alternative is to employ reputable merchant bankers who are known to specialize in investment abroad, but the investor must know enough of investment conditions abroad and individual overseas investments to be able to approve any recommendations put forward and to take an intelligent interest in what is happening.

I would not advise a *direct* participation in overseas equities in the case of a small trust or for a small investor. On the death of the beneficiary or the owner all kinds of difficulties arise. The death has to be proved in each country concerned – documents sworn before notaries – personal representatives appointed and issued with Powers of Attorney – death duties paid. The expenses are very heavy – in fact prohibitive for a small holding.

Then there is the investment dollar premium which has to be paid to secure foreign currency for investment overseas. The dollar premium varies daily. During the last twelve months it has been as high as 40 and is currently 25. (Both figures are after adjusting for the current exchange rate between Britain and the United States.)

It has to be remembered too that, on a sale of an overseas investment other than in the currency of countries in the sterling area at June 1972, 25 per cent. of the investment dollars converted at the current exchange rate have to be surrendered to the Bank of England for cash. This means that the dollar premium is lost on 25 per cent. of the proceeds.

### *Timing*

This demands not only skill, but in addition the ability to make decisions; the belief that it is right at that point of time to act. There is no doubt whatsoever that first class investments can be bought or sold at the wrong time. There is a time when investors temporarily neglect individual first class shares or alternatively over-chase them. There is always greater interest at dividend times or in anticipation of the accounts. The high and low points of some very sound shares can rarely be justified. It is the professional investor's aim to buy the shares when they are cheap and not when everyone is buying them.

Apart from this, no advice can be given on this matter of timing other than to keep up to date with the market and to observe all the factors which have been stressed earlier in the book. A number of systems have been devised based on indices and charts but, although charts are useful, only a few investors seem to follow any of the systems based on charts. Above all, I think a person close to the market frequently has an 'instinct' as to whether a share is dear or cheap.

One factor to be remembered where trustees are concerned is that a trustee is a continual investor. Because of the claims of his beneficiaries to income he cannot keep out of the market. In the following paragraph I touch upon the dangers of 'going liquid'. It is possible sometimes, however, to form a definite view as to the comparative investment prospects of gilts and equities. There are times when gilts appear to be over-valued as compared with equities and vice versa, and this gives some scope from time to time for adjusting the proportions of the fund in gilts and equities respectively.

*'Going Liquid'*

There is frequently talk of 'going liquid' although it is impracticable when income is of importance, but it comes much more from individual investors than from the professional. It implies realizing part or all of a portfolio and getting back into the constituent equities at appreciably lower levels. This is a very difficult operation, because it involves not only foretelling the future but also overcoming a 5 to 7 per cent. handicap. The 7 per cent. covers stamp duty, two lots of commission and the jobber's turn.

Suppose the *Financial Times* Industrial Share Index has touched a high point of 500 and starts to fall, and a decision to 'go liquid' is taken when the index has dropped to 470: that would be prompt action indeed. A 7 per cent. drop on 470 brings the index down to 437, and at that point the portfolio could in theory be repurchased without loss or profit. Obviously, a further 5 per cent. drop, taking the index to 415, is a minimum to make the trouble and worry worth while, and that is a total fall of 85 points from the high point. No portfolio is likely to be the same as the portfolio of the *Financial Times* index and will not necessarily follow the same course; in fact the professional investor would expect to beat the *Financial Times* index. A 15 per cent. fall in the *Financial Times* index therefore is unlikely to involve a similar fall in a carefully chosen portfolio.

There has been much pressure to 'go liquid' during the past ten years – many alarms and incursions – but many who have 'gone liquid' may well have regretted it. To succeed in 'going liquid' it is necessary to diagnose the ending of a bull market and the commencement of a bear market, to watch the bear market through its phases (the bear market of 1929 lasted twenty years) and then select the right time when a fall is succeeded by a rise which is repeated by a smaller fall and a larger rise, and so on.

Looking back over the years at the chart there seem to have been plenty of opportunities for 'going liquid', but when making the decision one is looking at a blank sheet of graph paper, reading a host of conflicting opinions and living in an atmosphere of uncertainty. It is very difficult, and most professional investment advisers will not readily support a suggestion to 'go liquid'. Their skill is directed more as to whether individual investments are dear or cheap; they are concerned with genuine investment.

Going liquid has become even more difficult when with Capital Gains Tax the only certain thing is the payment within a year of substantial Capital Gains Tax.

*Miscellaneous Points*

Here are some hints concerning investing:

(1) Keep in daily touch with the market.
(2) Make all decisions calmly: do not allow any adviser to rush you into action.
(3) Once you have made a decision, act quickly.
(4) Never be afraid to cut a loss.
(5) Do not be in a hurry to buy on an established falling market or to sell on an established rising market.
(6) Do not – and this advice should be taken to heart by all people who manage their own investments – fidget with your investments: buy good shares and try to forget them.
(7) When choosing a share, choose one which is basic and fundamental to the economy of the country – food, clothing, household goods. Avoid the shares of companies dealing with

luxuries, particularly at times of recession or incipient recession. Remember, a share becomes over-valued when too many chase its prospects. A share becomes under-valued when its difficulties are over-stressed or when its potentialities are not generally recognized.

(8) Remember that the stock exchange is a barometer of all market influences, a reflector of up-to-date stored knowledge. It sifts market gossip and crystallizes all factors in market values. The professional investor has a healthy respect for the stock exchange as a pricer of shares.

(9) Skim off the cream when a share has appreciated substantially and looks dear.

(10) Use the proceeds of (9) in further diversifying the portfolio.

(11) The principal attributes of a competent investor are a good memory, a long experience and shrewdness.

(12) My view is that little benefit is derived from so-called inside information. I am quite sure that some tips are 'planted'.

(13) It is a great mistake to allow long-term decisions to be influenced by passing events.

(14) A professional investor should seek as much advice and knowledge as he can assimilate, but he must be prepared to make up his own mind.

(15) Cultivate a healthy suspicion of the written word: 'a lengthy review of a share with a glossy cover is not necessarily accurate in every respect.

## CHAPTER 10

# Reviewing Investments

An essential part of the art of investment is the periodic review of portfolios and individual investments. Before reviewing a portfolio of investments it is desirable to prepare a valuation of the individual investments comprising the portfolio, grouping the investments on the lines suggested on pages 45 and 46. It is helpful, in the case of fixed-interest stocks, to list the stocks in ascending order of date. In the case of equities the valuation statement should give:

(a) nominal amount of holding; book value; market value;
(b) earnings and dividend yield per cent. for last two years;
(c) highest and lowest price in respect of the twelve months under review;
(d) current price and gross yield based on current price;
(e) price/earnings ratio (see p. 102).

Note (a) (b) (c) adjusted in respect of rights and bonus issues.

A large fund should be reviewed at least twice a year, but it would be sufficient to review a fund of modest size annually.

A review of a portfolio of investments which has been chosen by a competent investor and his advisers would not usually call for much action apart from:

(a) considering whether there has been any change in the circumstances of the fund or the trust or the beneficiaries which makes it desirable to modify the investment policy; estate duty is always a problem with personal trusts and it becomes urgent to deal with this impending liability when a life tenant grows old. Four per cent. Victory Bonds can be tendered at par for estate duty purposes provided they have been held for six months, and if they can be purchased well below par they are well worth buying;
(b) considering very carefully the respective proportions of the fund in fixed-interest stocks and equities, and whether current

conditions require some adjustment between the two (see page 40);

(c) considering the distribution under the various groups and whether adjustment between the groups is desirable;

(d) reducing the amount of those holdings which have shown remarkable growth and now represent too large a proportion of the fund and investing the proceeds in other investments, thereby achieving further diversification;

(e) reflecting whether there has been any change in the standing of any investment or in its prospects;

(f) selling any investment which is not showing the growth expected of it – this requires courage;

(g) looking for capital gains losses to set against profits.

The object of a review is not merely to confirm that in many ways the fund has been invested successfully, but to probe the weaknesses of the fund and to deal with them. In particular, trustees must resist 'changes' for the sake of change. Buying and selling securities is expensive; there are, as already mentioned, the jobber's turn both ways, stamp duty and commission.

*Book Value*

In the first edition of this book, I wrote that there are many investors who criticize the keeping of book values and I went on to argue that book values should not influence a decision except from the taxation aspect of profit or loss. However, I believed then and still believe that they nevertheless have a useful function in that they spotlight the investor's mistakes or lack of success. A fund invested in ten equities might in the course of the years double its value – not an unsatisfactory performance – but an inspection of the book values might reveal the fact that three of the investments in the portfolio have performed very indifferently. Since the advent of Capital Gains Tax all investors must keep not only a note of book values but actual cost.

*Testing Portfolio Performance*

Many investors and in particular the institutional investors will want to know how their fund has performed as compared with the market as a whole.

There are a variety of performance tests based on share indices. I prefer the *F.T.* Actuaries Indices and in its simplest form the test for a fund which has had *no* new money put into it during the period under review is a straight comparative performance with the appropriate indices. Where, however, new money has gone into the fund the simplest check is hypothetically to buy, with the value of the fund at the beginning of the review period, units of the appropriate *F.T.* Actuaries Indices and, as the new money comes in, to invest the money in the appropriate indices at the appropriate dates; then at the end of the period under review to value the total *F.T.* Actuaries units representing the fund at the end of the period and to compare the performance of the hypothetical fund with the actual fund. Percentages will show which has done better. There is a lengthy chapter on this highly technical subject in another of my books, *Principles of Pension Fund Investment*, published by Hutchinson.

CHAPTER 11

# Investment Trusts

*Nature and History*

An investment trust is a company which invests its share and loan capital almost entirely in marketable investments. The object is to get together a sound portfolio of investments which will provide the company's equity shareholders with increasing dividends and capital appreciation. Investment trusts have pioneered the art of diversification.

*Definition*

I rather like the description of an investment trust which appeared some time ago in the *Stock Exchange Gazette*: 'It is a limited company which uses the capital subscribed by its shareholders to purchase shares in other companies. The object is to hold these shares as fixed assets with a view to obtaining a gradually increasing income. But just as an industrial company may, from time to time, dispose of plant and machinery that is not fully productive, so may an investment trust sell one investment and buy another, which seems to offer better prospects. Many industrial companies issue preference capital and debenture stock, thereby borrowing money at a fixed rate of interest. This fixed interest capital is used to buy assets which will eventually produce an income greater than the interest on the money which has been borrowed (the Gearing factor). Likewise, an investment trust will borrow funds in the same way and for the same purpose. At first the return may be less than the interest on the borrowed money, but once the fixed-interest dividends have been covered any further increase is profit for the ordinary shareholders alone.'

The term investment trust is somewhat misleading. These companies are really investment companies but so are many other companies which are grouped under other headings. The term investment trust implies trusteeship whereas the relationship of the directors to the shareholders is the same as any other company – that of quasi-trust only – not that of trustee and beneficiary. They have been called investment trusts for ninety years and to change such an historical name would in my view lead to confusion.

According to returns made to the Bank of England, 266 investment trusts held assets as at 31st December, 1972, to a total value of £7,456 million. In a lecture to the Insurance Institute of London on 11th October, 1961, Mr D. A. Pease, A.C.A., stated that twelve years previously the assets were worth less than £800 million and that of the growth during the twelve-year period, retained profits had contributed some £50 million, and new issues £158 million, but by far the bulk of the increase came from capital appreciation in the assets held.

The total number of individual holdings varies with each trust. There are some large trusts with approximately 400 and one that at one time had 1,000 and more. One trust of £30 million limits the number to about 250 taking the view that there are a limited number of first class companies, further that the time factor puts a ceiling on the amount of effective supervision which can be undertaken and that an excessive number of holdings merely buys the performance of equities in general.

Investment trusts are not as popular with investors as a whole as they should be. In the nature of things the investment trust pursues its efficient way rather unseen. Little press advertising, no television programmes, yet their investment achievements are outstanding. In general the trusts are under expert management and the expenses of running them are low – generally from 4 to 5 per cent. of the gross income. Put another way, the expenses of the fifty investment trusts included in the *F.T.* Actuaries Index represent 0·14 per cent. of total asset value.

*First-class Performance*

Clearly investment trusts have resoundingly beaten the performance of equities as a whole. This has been demonstrated many times and no better than in a stockbrokers' pamphlet which showed the value, at the end of May 1961, of £100 invested at the end of 1952 in each of the following media:

| | |
|---|---|
| (a) U.K. fixed-interest securities .. .. | 82 |
| (b) U.K. industrial equities .. .. .. | 304 |
| (c) American common stocks .. .. | 226 |
| (d) U.K. investment trust equities .. .. | 672 |

Adjusting these figures to the current indices (14.8.73) the corresponding figures are:

(a) £62 (b) £354 (c) £399 (d) £1,121

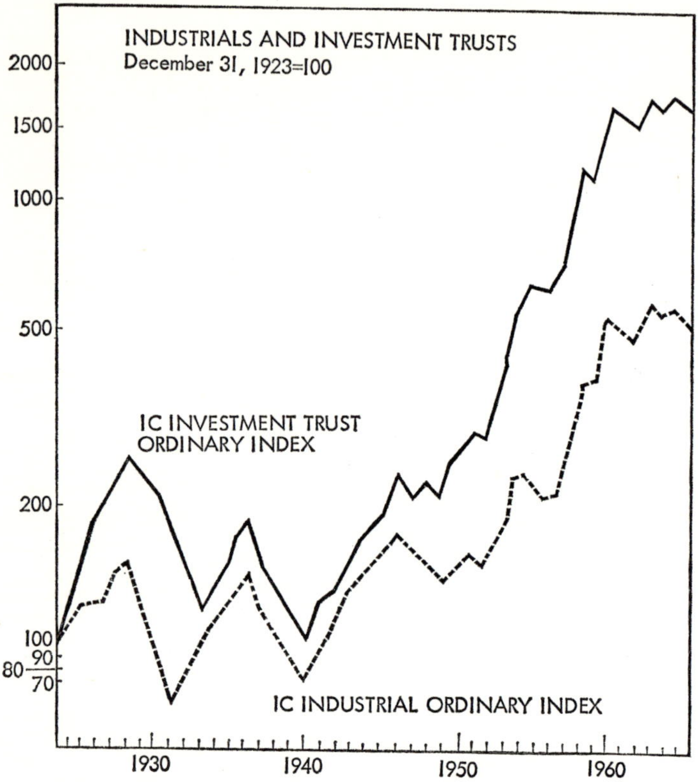


Performance of Investment Trusts compared with Ordinary Shares (*Investors' Chronicle* indices), 1923 to 1966

Reproduced by courtesy of *Investors' Chronicle Ltd*

Here are some figures extracted from the *Investors' Chronicle* (15.7.60) showing the value then of £100 invested at various purchase dates. Note especially that the purchase dates vary considerably:

Performance of Investment Trusts and Ordinary Shares
(*Financial Times* Actuaries Indices), 1967 to 1973

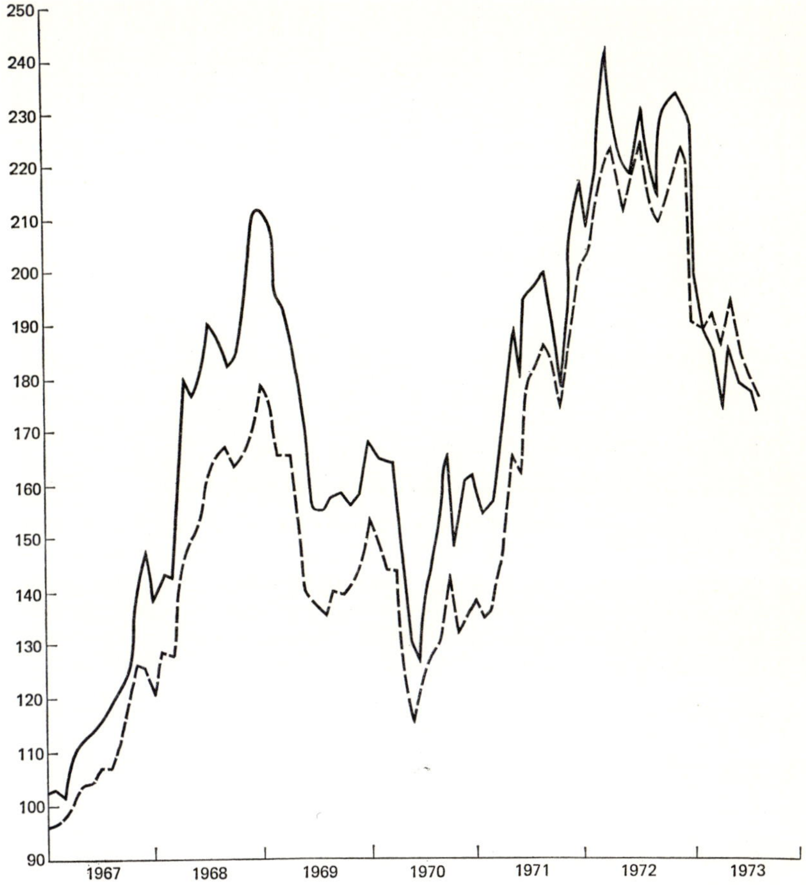


Note unbroken line refers to F.T.A. Investment Trust Index.
Broken line refers to F.T.A. All Share Index.

| *Trust* | *Purchase date* | *price* 15.7.60. s. d. | *value* 15.7.60. £ | *Annual appreciation* %* |
|---|---|---|---|---|
| A. .. .. .. .. | June 1946 | 55 6 | 830 | 17 |
| B. .. .. .. .. | 1948 | 12 0 | 960 | 21 |
| C. .. .. .. .. | 1950 (a) | 16 0 | 500 | Over 17 |
| D. .. .. .. .. | Jan. 1949 | 20 6 | 400 | 12 |
| E. .. .. .. .. | Jan. 1949 | 525 0 | 1,630 | 27 |
| F. .. .. .. .. | Mar. 1951 | 23 0 | 490 | 19 |
| G. .. .. .. .. | June 1946 | 20 3 | 790 | 16 |
| H. .. .. .. .. | Jan. 1949 | 240 0 | 1,850 | 32 |
| I. .. .. .. .. | 1873 | 96 3 | 30,800 | 7 |
| J. .. .. .. .. | 1934 | 96 3 | 1,540 | 11 |
| K. .. .. .. .. | Jan. 1949 | — | 1,460 | 8 |
| *Investors' Chronicle* Index .. | Dec. 1923 | 20 6 | 430 | 15 |

* Since purchase date. (*a*) Original investment £73; a further £27 invested on various dates. In the meantime (14.8.73) the Investment Trust Indices has gone up by 137 per cent.

The graphs on pp. 76 and 77 show how excellently investment trusts have fared as compared with equities generally.

From a booklet issued by a firm of stockbrokers I have culled the following in respect of the ten-year period to 31.12.58:

*Investors' Chronicle* index of industrial shares – a rise of 1·9 times.
Investments trust equities – a rise of 4·1 times.

According to a booklet issued by the Association of Investment Trust Companies, an investment made on 30th June, 1962 in the fifty companies comprising the *F.T.* Actuaries Investment Trust Index would have increased on average by over 150 per cent. by 30th June, 1972, and the income received from the investment would have risen by over 80 per cent.

*Advantages*

Investment trusts have some unique attractions:

(A) *Diversification*

Investment trusts are the premier exponents of diversification in equity investment. Here are some figures extracted from the accounts of an investment trust:

(a) *Geographical spread*

| | % |
|---|---|
| Great Britain .. .. | 76·66 |
| Commonwealth (excluding Canada) .. .. | 7·25 |
| North America .. .. | 11·97 |
| Other countries .. .. | 4·12 |
| | 100·00 |

(b) *Classification of investments*

| | % |
|---|---|
| Debentures .. .. | 1·75 |
| Preference .. .. | 6·55 |
| Equities .. .. | 91·70 |
| | 100·00 |

(c) *Number of holdings* .. 890

(d) *Book value of investments* .. £3,561,779

(e) *Market value* .. £9,168,766

(f) *Analysis of investments at valuation*

| | No. of securities | Value at £ | % |
|---|---|---|---|
| Foreign Governments and Corporations .. | 10 | 1,102 | 0·01 |
| Banks .. .. .. .. .. .. | 22 | 271,919 | 2·96 |
| Breweries, Distilleries & Wine Merchants .. | 25 | 411,093 | 4·48 |
| Building & Civil Engineering: | | | |
| (i) Contractors and Plant .. .. | 25 | 180,329 | 1·97 |
| (ii) Materials and Components .. .. | 35 | 280,155 | 3·05 |
| Chemicals and Plastics .. .. .. | 28 | 371,456 | 4·05 |
| Engineering: | | | |
| (i) Heavy Electrical .. .. .. | 13 | 91,338 | 0·99 |
| (ii) Light Electrical, Radio & Records .. | 39 | 375,052 | 4·09 |
| (iii) Shipbuilding, Boilermaking & General Engineering .. .. | 50 | 481,015 | 5·25 |
| (iv) Specialist Engineering .. .. | 42 | 280,320 | 3·06 |
| (v) Machine Tools, Metal Manufacturers & Merchants .. .. .. | 48 | 493,622 | 5·38 |
| (vi) Office Equipment .. .. .. | 8 | 219,734 | 2·40 |
| Finance and Hire Purchase .. .. .. | 18 | 166,448 | 1·81 |
| Food and Tobacco .. .. .. .. | 34 | 292,948 | 3·20 |
| Hotels, Catering & Entertainment .. .. | 8 | 74,908 | 0·82 |
| Industrial Holding Companies .. .. | 15 | 279,148 | 3·04 |
| Insurance .. .. .. .. .. | 16 | 652,074 | 7·11 |
| Investment Trusts .. .. .. .. | 40 | 1,041,148 | 11·36 |
| Land and Pastoral .. .. .. .. | 10 | 64,721 | 0·71 |
| Merchanting and Warehousing .. .. | 12 | 81,717 | 0·90 |
| Mines: | | | |
| (i) Gold Mines & Mining Finance Cos. | 12 | 87,135 | 0·95 |
| (ii) Other Mines .. .. .. .. | 22 | 102,749 | 1·12 |
| Motors, Aircraft & Components .. .. | 32 | 243,576 | 2·66 |
| Oil and Natural Gas Producers and Distributors .. .. .. .. .. | 30 | 351,459 | 3·83 |
| Packaging .. .. .. .. .. | 12 | 75,023 | 0·82 |
| Paper, Printing & Publishing .. .. | 34 | 243,741 | 2·66 |
| Plantation Companies: | | | |
| (i) Rubber .. .. .. .. | 17 | 100,177 | 1·09 |
| (ii) Other .. .. .. .. .. | 10 | 35,542 | 0·39 |
| Real Property .. .. .. .. | 22 | 242,008 | 2·64 |
| Shipping .. .. .. .. .. | 16 | 148,419 | 1·62 |
| Steel .. .. .. .. .. .. | 18 | 224,532 | 2·45 |
| Stores, Furniture and Shoes .. .. | 51 | 452,228 | 4·93 |
| Textiles: | | | |
| (i) Cotton and Artificial .. .. | 11 | 60,591 | 0·66 |
| (ii) Wool and Carpets .. .. .. | 15 | 70,135 | 0·77 |
| (iii) Other .. .. .. .. .. | 14 | 97,327 | 1·06 |
| Transport .. .. .. .. .. | 14 | 91,509 | 1·00 |
| Utilities .. .. .. .. .. | 27 | 219,731 | 2·39 |
| Miscellaneous .. .. .. .. | 21 | 212,637 | 2·32 |
| | 890 | 9,168,766 | 100·00 |

The Alliance Trust, one of the largest trusts, had the following spread of investments according to the last account. Note the high proportion in the U.S.A.

(a) *Geographical spread*

| | % |
|---|---|
| Great Britain .. .. | 61·5 |
| Commonwealth.. .. | — |
| U.S.A. .. .. .. | 35·4 |
| Other countries .. .. | 3·1 |
| | 100·0 |

(b) *Classification of investments*

| | % |
|---|---|
| Fixed-interest .. | 7·2 |
| Equities .. .. | 92·8 |
| | 100·0 |

(B) *Earnings covered amply by Earnings of Portfolio Equities*

The income the investment trust receives by way of dividends from companies whose equities are comprised in its portfolios was, before the advent of Corporation Tax, covered about twice. The earnings in 1960 for example of the component securities of the trust referred to above totalled £651,808 and the dividends paid £330,096. (These are unfortunately 1960 figures and the company did not give the information in subsequent years.) It will, however, be noted that at the time there was a hidden cover of 1·97 times the trust revenue. This is the first cushion. Following the change to Corporation Tax in 1965, the cover fell somewhat. It has more recently recovered owing to an increase in the earnings of the companies whose shares are held by the investment trusts and to the governmental restriction in dividend payments.

Under the new system of Corporation Tax the cover is likely to increase further.

(C) *Investment Trusts retain about 15 per cent. of gross Earnings for Reinvestment*

On an average, investment trusts distribute only about 85 per cent. of their earnings, the balance being ploughed back and reinvested. Here is another cushion. (*N.B.* – A good point for the high taxpayer, too.)

(D) *Gearing Factor*

Most investment trusts have borrowed money on prior charges and some at low rates of interest. This money is in the main invested in equities. If a trust requires £*x* to meet the interest on its debenture stock and preference shares and its net earnings are £500,000, this sum less £$x$ is available for its ordinary shareholders and all additional income it receives inures for the benefit of its ordinary shareholders. Assuming £$x$ to be £50,000 and that the following year the trust income goes up by 10 per cent. and that the trust retains 20 per cent. of its net income and distributes the rest, we get the following position:

| | *Current year* | *Following year* |
|---|---|---|
| | £ | £ |
| Net earnings .. .. | 500,000 | 550,000 |
| Fixed charges .. .. | 50,000 | 50,000 |
| | 450,000 | 500,000 |
| Income retained .. .. | 90,000 | 100,000 |
| | £360,000 | £400,000 |

Percentage increase in following year paid as dividend to shareholders: approx. 11 per cent.

Some investment trusts are described as having a low gearing (a small proportion of loan capital and preference shares) and others as having a high gearing. While income is rising, the ordinary shareholder of a trust with a high gearing is on a good wicket, but if the trust goes through a period of reducing income the shareholder of the low-geared trust is obviously in a comparatively better position. The effect of gearing is lessened when the trust is paying a high rate of interest on its prior capital and is negated where an amount more or less equivalent to its prior charges is invested in fixed-interest securities at a similar rate of interest.

Similarly, gearing affects the asset value of an investment trust share. If there is significant debenture, preference and other fixed-interest capital a change in the value of the investment trust's funds will cause a proportionately higher change in the breakup value of the trust's ordinary shares. The shareholder is in a happy position with rising share values but is in a poorer position, compared with a lowly geared share, when markets fall.

(E) At the present time the market values of the portfolios of investment trusts are greatly in excess of book values – see figures on page 82.

(F) *Excess of Breakup Value of Shares over Market Value*

To quote from a paper I wrote in May 1961, for the Annual Conference of the Chartered Institute of Secretaries:

'The fact that the market price of an investment trust share is usually less than the breakup value taking the portfolio of investments at market prices is another cushion which softens the risk taken by the shareholder of an investment trust. It is generally taken for granted that investment trust shares have this cushion. To put it another way, when an investor purchases an investment trust share he almost invariably buys the share at a *discount* as compared with its breakup value. One leading firm of stockbrokers refers to the surplus as the *depreciation percentage* – namely, the amount by which the value of the portfolio allowing for gearing has to fall before the surplus disappears. Here are some examples.

| *Trust* | *Market price* | *Breakup value* | *Depreciation* | *Discount* |
|---|---|---|---|---|
| | p | p | % | % |
| 'A' .. .. | 92 | 112½ | 15 | 18 |
| 'B' .. .. | 95 | 120 | 18 | 21 |
| 'C' .. .. | 42 | 61½ | 29 | 32 |

'This discount or depreciation percentage puzzles me a little – it means that, apart from a few investment trusts, management is at a discount – nothing paid for proved successful management. Shares in a sound portfolio available at less than the proportionate cost of the underlying securities. I would expect the discount eventually to disappear except for any trusts whose record is uninspiring.'

My predictions proved to be all too true: the discounts did disappear for a number of top trusts, indeed some trusts established premiums. However, the discount position has varied from time to time and at present (autumn 1973) the discounts have become substantial again following the uncertainties of the equity market.

(G) *Portfolio Extends to North American Market, etc.*

Another advantage of the investment trust is that it is an excellent means of acquiring an interest in the North American market, and eventually too, and already to some extent, in Common Market stocks. Some trusts have 40 to 50 per cent. of their funds in American common stocks. This can involve paying the investment dollar premium (see page 67).

By arranging special 'back-to-back' loans in which a sterling deposit is matched with a foreign currency loan, investment trusts can largely avoid paying the dollar premium on foreign holdings. These facilities are available only to the institutional investor or to the largest private investors.

(H) *Taxation*

Since 1972 investment trusts have been liable to pay Corporation Tax at only 15 per cent. on net realized capital gains; the previous rate was 30 per cent. Under the old system holders received certificates of apportionment showing the capital gains paid by the trust apportioned to their share holding. The total of the capital gains paid as shown in the certificates could effectively be set off against the gains realized should the investor sell his shares.

Under the new system shareholders in investment trusts and investors in unit trusts receive a 15 per cent. Capital Gains Tax credit to set against their capital gains liability on the sale of their holdings. Furthermore an individual can elect to pay, at his option, annual gains up to £5,000 at half his top rate of tax. Thus someone liable to income tax at the basic rate of 30 per cent. would only pay capital gains at 15 per cent. and in the case of profits from the sale of investment trusts and unit trusts the 15 per cent. credit would wipe out the gains for capital gains purposes. The new system, therefore, is extremely advantageous to investment trusts and unit trust investors.

On the income side, investment trusts pay Corporation Tax on unfranked income (see page 99) to the extent that it exceeds management and other expenses including debenture and loan interest (but not preference dividends). As many trusts receive considerable unfranked income from their overseas investments, they suffered a significant setback on the change to Corporation Tax. Dividends from U.K. equity and preference shares are, of course, franked for Corporation Tax and no further tax is payable provided the dividends are distributed by the trust. On the other hand, interest on their investment of debentures and loan stocks, being paid from profits before Corporation Tax, is not franked and is thus subject to Corporation Tax in the hands of the investment trust, unless expenses and the interest on the trust's own indebtedness covers it.

Under the new imputation system of Corporation Tax (which will be described fully in a later chapter), the basic principles remain the same, although the relative advantage of franked income as compared with unfranked income is lessened, where this income is distributed as dividend, in view of the lower overall rate of Corporation Tax that will be paid, after allowing for the offsetting of Advance Corporation Tax (see page 102) against the main Corporation Tax charge.

It took Investment Trusts a few years to adjust their portfolios of investment to the incidence of Corporation Tax by acquiring the right amount of franked income.

Like other companies liable to Corporation Tax, the dividends on the preference share capital of an investment trust have to be paid out of income which has suffered Corporation Tax – unlike the interest on loan capital which can be deducted before calculating the amount of profit chargeable to Corporation Tax. It does not look as if investment trusts will raise any preference capital in the future; indeed they may even take the necessary steps to repay their preference capital.

Contrariwise, preference shares being franked for income tax and Corporation Tax are, all other things being acceptable, suitable for the investment of the funds of investment trusts. Not so loan capital interest, which is unfranked for Corporation Tax.

*Less Favourable Factors*

*Marketability of Shares below Average* – As I see it, the only objection of any substance to investment trust shares is that they are not as marketable as some investors would wish. If the investor is buying, the chances are that there is not sufficient stock available, and if he is selling when markets are bad it is much more difficult to sell investment trust shares than market leaders. Investment trust managers appear to be tackling this problem. There have been more investment trust amalgamations in the past few years or so than I can ever remember: there are trusts now with over 10,000 shareholders.

Some trusts are splitting down their shares into smaller denominations. Both these factors should increase marketability. Instead of the slow process of securing more members through rights issues, one trust bravely went to the market a few years ago and made an issue of shares at a price equivalent to the proportionate value of the securities comprising the trust portfolio at the time of the issue. Despite a not particularly favourable press which I thought was a little unfair (the trust was doing no more than the unit trust movement does in extending its business), the trust by this operation increased its shareholders more than tenfold, to 3,500, and in so doing improved the market in the shares for the benefit of all its shareholders. Some years later, according to its annual report, the number of shareholders had risen to 7,324.

To sum up, over half the trusts have assets of £10 million or less. Of the larger ones twenty-one only have on the average two Stock Exchange dealings per day. Here are some details of six of the largest, all of which were established before 1890, where it is possible daily to buy up to £5,000 worth of shares:

| | *Assets* | *Price* (14.8.73) | *Yield* |
|---|---|---|---|
| | £m. | p | % |
| Alliance .. .. .. | 120 | 184 | 3·4 |
| Foreign & Colonial .. .. | 136 | 150 | 2·0 |
| Industrial & General .. | 129 | 40½ | 3·7 |
| Mercantile .. .. .. | 119 | 53½ | 4·2 |
| Globe .. .. .. .. | 125 | 83 | 3·7 |
| British Investment .. .. | 128 | 157 | 2·6 |

The advent of Corporation Tax hit investment trusts because under Corporation Tax, unlike under income tax, the tax borne on overseas investments could not be set off against tax due in this country. In order to soften the blow, there was some transitional relief, but it was soon used up by investment trusts. The change affected the growth in investment trust earnings seriously, a blow from which they are only now recovering.

Obviously prior to the advent of Corporation Tax investment trusts with their heavy overseas investments had low net U.K. rates (see page 105). Thus, the shares were not suitable to the small investor paying little or no tax, or to charities and pension funds.

With the disappearance of the net U.K. rate investment trust shares can be fully recommended to all investors including the small investor and to all gross funds – that is funds which are not liable to tax.

I can remember long periods when investment trust portfolios were worth substantially less than their book values; in fact, all has not always been well in the investment trust movement, and in the late 1930s several articles appeared in the financial papers drawing attention to poor results. But since then the trusts seem to have unobtrusively and efficiently reorganized themselves.

Since 1952 investment trusts have been basking in the equity boom. As the table on page 78 shows, the large majority of the trusts were operating before 1950 and in consequence they benefited from all the stored-up income and reserves of the 1939 to 1950 period (voluntary dividend limitation, results of the easing of wartime taxation) which eventually flowed from the investments in the companies comprising their portfolios. In my opinion, investment trusts are unlikely to produce in the future results of the exceptional order of the past fifteen years or so, but the average investor is unlikely to beat the performance of the well-managed investment trust; in fact, the professional investor will have to use all his skill and imagination to select a portfolio to beat the perhaps over-diversified portfolio of the investment trust.

A number of stockbrokers specialize in investment trusts. These include Myers & Co., Norris Oakley Brothers, Laing & Cruickshank, Phillips & Drew, James Capel & Co., L. Messel & Co., Hoare & Co., Govett, Wood MacKenzie.

CHAPTER 12

# Unit Trusts

*Description and Historical*

A unit trust is an invested fund of stocks and shares divided into equal units of a prescribed amount. The units belong to the unit holders in proportion to the amount of money subscribed by them. The object of the trust is in the first place to enable the small investor (though the big investor is also welcomed) to have an interest in a large spread of investment with experienced selection and supervision and with complete security. A unit trust, unlike an investment trust, is not a company incorporated under the Companies Acts but an association of investors. Thus an investment trust's affairs are managed by its directors while the affairs of a unit trust are under the care of an *ad hoc* management company which also acts as the market for purchases and sales of units, an independent trustee being responsible for security arrangements.

The movement is active in most, if not all, the large nations of the world. The British movement to begin with restricted itself to United Kingdom equities, but now there are many trusts that specialize in American, European and other overseas shares.

The unit trust movement started in the United Kingdom in 1931. By March 1939, their investments had totalled £80 million. Little progress was made during the war years or for some time after, owing mainly to restrictions on capital issues.

*Progress*

At the time the first edition of this book went to press, I gave the figures of the movement as at 31st October, 1962 and predicted a rosy future for the movement. Then the number of trusts was 54; there were 785,000 unit holders and the value of the funds involved amounted to £255,115,785. The extent of the increase since then can be judged from the figures at the end of July 1973 when total funds had increased to £2,500 million. The number of trusts had grown to over 300 and the number of unit holders, of which of course there is some duplication, had increased to 2,269,536, while the average holding had gone up from £343 to £1,094. It was a great victory for the movement when Lloyds Bank Limited launched its own unit trust in October 1966, and later other banks and the insurance companies followed.

The multiplicity of the number and types of unit trusts must be confusing to the layman. I certainly do not find it easy myself to keep up with the variety of methods which are used or the various gimmicks which are introduced from time to time to popularize them. The prospective unit holder now, it seems to me, needs the advice of an equivalent of an insurance broker to advise him of the type of trust best suited to his needs. I certainly regard the innovation of door-to-door salesman as dangerous.

This growth has resulted from:

(1) extensively advertised block issues;
(2) the cult of the equity;
(3) the ingenuity of the movement in finding more and more ways of presenting equity investment to the public and in particular linking life assurance to regular savings, under which the subscriber secures the life assurance rebate on the amount saved annually.

Here is one example: for a man aged forty, subject to the basic rate of tax, paying £100 per annum for twenty years (the younger man does better still):

| | £ |
|---|---|
| Annual subscription .. .. .. .. .. .. | 100·00 |
| Income tax relief at 30p in the £ on one-half of subscription | 15·00 |
| Net annual outlay .. .. .. .. .. .. | 85·00 |

Total net outlay over the twenty-year period is £85 × 20 = £1,700. Ten pounds of the subscription goes in administration purposes, including the life assurance cover, and the balance of £90 is invested in units together with the half-yearly income.

The illustration which one unit trust provides *assumes* a possible increase in the value of the units of 5½ per cent. per annum, representing 'an average increase in value of units over the term of 3 per cent. per annum and net distributions at the rate of 2½ per cent. per annum on the value of units from time to time', thus giving a value at the end of the twenty-year term of £3,410.

When this scheme came out some two years ago I criticized one aspect, namely that there was no guaranteed amount at the end of the twenty-year savings period. A number of groups have since met this criticism. The amount guaranteed at the end of the savings period (and apparently this applies now to all their past life schemes) is the total net cash invested for the subscriber. There could hardly be a better way of buying equities except for buying first class investment trusts at a discount.

Considerable additional success has been achieved by expanding into the field of trusts for children, including those made by both grandparents and parents, another example of the ingenuity of the managers.

The equity-linked contract was pioneered by the London & Edinburgh Life Insurance Company, a relatively small company.

When unit trust managers realized the selling potential of the contract there was a rush to get their own contracts going. For this purpose the majority established their own *ad hoc* life companies. A few used the services of existing life companies linking their units as investments for the equity-linked life policies issued.

Later the ever inventive unit trusts management groups issued varying types of bonds through their associated life companies. Indeed, their attractions led to the old established life companies joining the hunt for this very profitable business. It had also taxation advantages for the issuing life company.

The two main types of bonds are the guaranteed income bond (it's as well to weigh up the value of the guarantee), whereby a high rate of interest of around 9 per cent. free of tax at the basic rate was guaranteed for five to ten years with your money back at the end of the period.

Another is the annuity bond, where the income was accumulated at a high rate of interest.

The snag for the high taxpayer is that he is liable to tax in excess of the basic rate of 30 per cent. when the bond is repaid. The liability is calculated by ascertaining the amount received in excess of the amount paid. The difference is divided by the number of years the bond has been in force. The resulting figure is added to the bond-holder's income to arrive at his top rate of tax and this rate less 30 per cent. is then applied to the whole of the difference. Example: proceeds of a 10 year bond, £2,500; total paid, £1,000; surplus £1,500. Add £150 to decide rate tax. Assume tax rate 5%. (50 − 30 = 20) Additional tax, £1,500 at 20% = £300.

These bonds are sometimes linked to the issuing life company's funds, which can be a normal life or one based on the units of a unit trust, or property or gilt-edged securities or an amalgam of these.

Considerable concern has been expressed from time to time regarding the methods adopted by some salesmen of unit trust linked policies.

The Insurance Amendment Act, 1973, which embodies some of the recommendations of the Hillary Scott committee, should go a long way to removing any abuses, but before things can be tightened up the required regulations will have to be formulated by the D.T.I. These will include a waiting period of ten days during which the assured can cancel his proposal for his policy. The D.T.I. will also prescribe regulations for future advertising.

While things are in temporary limbo one doubts whether any insurer would flout the clear spirit and objectives of the Act.

*Investment portfolios*

The portfolios of unit trusts cover a wide field of investment. A minority of trusts have produced specialized investment portfolios in various ways, some have portfolios more or less exclusively consisting of the shares of (a) insurance companies, (b) investment trusts, (c) banks, (d) a mixture of (a), (b) and (c), and some (e) American and other foreign investments. By far the majority of the portfolios, however, are made up of a wide selection of British equities in industrial, financial, and commercial companies. In a short reference to unit trusts it is not possible to list the portfolio construction of the various trusts. Some trusts are designed mainly to provide a high current income yield, others are concerned with growth of capital and thus give a low current yield. Some have 40 investments, whilst one, I know, has as many as 180 investments. The average portfolio consists of about 100. Some trusts have a panel of investment experts to advise on their portfolios.

*Special-purpose Unit Trusts*

Although the majority of the trusts are designed for the small investor, there are some trusts which cater especially for various groups of investors. Thus there are unit trusts for pension funds, charities, trade unions and individual personal and family trusts. In fact the Trustee Investments Act both encourages and recognizes unit trusts as investments for the wider range fund.

It is a fundamental principle of the unit trust movement that the managers will buy back the units. It can thus be said that unit trusts have a ready market. Most trusts will send the proceeds of sale within a few days of receiving the unit certificate duly discharged.

When the movement started, unit trusts were termed 'fixed trusts' by reason of the fact that the portfolio of investments was fixed more or less irrevocably at the commencement of the trust; thus the unit holder knew exactly the shares in which he was taking an interest. Later, managers moved towards flexibility and the newer trusts gradually became more and more flexible.

*The Small Saver*

The literature of the movement is directed at the small saver. It must be remembered, however, that the realistic value of the unit will vary with the value of their underlying investments. In other words the market price will have its troughs and peaks. It would be wrong therefore for a small investor to put all his money into unit trusts – they are not suitable for moneys which he may need at short notice. Therefore he should not buy unit trust units until he has sufficient money for eventualities, in say National Savings Certificates, building societies, Post Office, and trustee savings banks, and the like; also adequate life assurance cover. In fairness to the unit trust movement this very point is often stressed in their literature. The fact that in times of falling prices there has not been an unmanageable rush to encash units suggests that they are fairly solidly held and the warning in this paragraph has been taken to heart.

*Trust Deed*

A unit trust must be secured by a trust deed approved by the Department of Trade and Industry, formerly called the Board of Trade. Thus a unit trust has a trustee – a bank or insurance company – and a management company. The D.T.I.'s powers stem from the schedule to the Prevention of Fraud (Investments) Acts, 1958, and these powers are exercised through D.T.I. requirements.

The trust deed must provide for:

(a) the calculation of the manager's prices for the units on a sale and a purchase respectively, and the yield from the units;
(b) the mode of execution and the issue of unit certificates: no units may be issued until the underlying investments have been vested in the trustee;
(c) every advertisement, circular, or other document containing

any statement with respect to the sale price of units, must state the yield from the units; such an advertisement, etc., must be approved by the trustee before issue;

(d) a fund, for defraying the expenses of the administration of the trust, must be established;

(e) accounts relating to the trust (including accounts of the management company in relation to the trust and statements of its remuneration) must be audited.

A trustee can require the retirement of the management company (subject to any provisions as to appeal contained in the deed) if the trustee certifies that it is in the interest of the unit holders.

*Operation*

The term of the trust is commonly twenty years, but the trust deed provides for an extension with the consent of the unit holders.

As already mentioned, the trustee has custody of the investments and the securities are registered in the trustee's name. The trustee acts as registrar and, in addition, is responsible for seeing that the terms of the trust deed are observed, that the unit certificates are issued, that no unauthorized investment is purchased and that the dividends are duly collected and distributed.

The charges for management vary among the different trusts. The D.T.I. regulates the charges that managers may make for the services they perform. I am informed by the Association of Unit Trust Managers that, over a twenty-year life of a trust, the maximum charge that managers are permitted currently to make is a total of 13¼ per cent. This is taken by way of an initial service charge often 5 per cent. (which is included in the cost price of a unit) and a semi-annual service charge levied on the value of the fund and taken either out of income or capital. From these charges the managers have to defray all the expenses of the trust (including the trustee's remuneration) and commissions to agents.

Income is usually distributed half-yearly; details of the make-up of the dividend distributions, including a list of the investments of the trust, are sent with the dividend payment to the unit holders together with income tax credit certificates.

The Finance Act, 1960 permitted the managers for the first time to set their management charges against the gross income of the trust instead of as previously the net income. Now that Corporation Tax has replaced income tax it is most desirable that all the income of a trust is already franked for Corporation Tax. This has resulted in British government stocks and loan stocks being unsuitable to a unit trust portfolio as such income is not franked for Corporation Tax. This is a disadvantage when equities are depressed. The benefit which the trusts secured under the Finance Act, 1960 is demonstrated by the fact that one trust reported that its effect was to increase the yields of its trust by approximately 30p.

Obviously the yield on the trust units will depend on the type of portfolio chosen. Some portfolios are chosen mainly with an eye to growth: others with the object of securing as high an income as is compatible with security; others mix growth stocks with the high yielders. At the time this was written the lowest yield was nil, and the highest yield 9·5 per cent.

Units may be purchased through a bank, the offices of the trustee, through stockbrokers, accountants and solicitors, or from the management company, and likewise sales are arranged through the same agencies. Prices of units are quoted in the daily papers. The value of a unit is based upon the value of the underlying securities plus stamp duty, settlement duty, brokers' commission and the initial service charge divided by the number of units in issue. The buying and selling prices are daily calculated in accordance with D.T.I. regulations and certified by a member firm of the London Stock Exchange.

Unit trusts advertise in the press and on television. One trust launched a block offer in January 1960, so successfully that in a few days £7 million was subscribed by approximately 60,000 investors and on 4th March, 1972 Lloyds Bank Second Fund brought in £10 millions. Unit trusts are bound to advertise if they are to extend their business by block offers, but it does mean that the advertising will bring in a few inexperienced investors who could get impatient if results are not quickly achieved. One group had advertised to calm the nerves of this type of investor. The movement does everything it can to ensure the proprieties, exhorting the public, but sometimes in very small print, to get their quota of National Savings Certificates before purchasing units, and managements mention in their block offer advertisements that the underlying securities can decrease in value as well as increase.

Nevertheless, I am somewhat concerned as to the reactions of the public to some of the advertisements for block issues as they do tend to leave the investor with the impression that the ensuing ten years may not differ widely from the last ten years or so, an assumption which in my view is not likely to be proved correct particularly for those unit holders who buy their units at the top of an equity boom.

*The Future*

As previously mentioned the unit trust principle is recognized in the Trustees Investments Act, and municipal and other corporations are encouraged to form their own unit trusts. There is a lot to be said for a panel of investments under the care of experts, carefully chosen, constantly under review and changed appropriately from time to time. There are some who would have preferred the Trustee Investments Act to have stipulated for a government-selected panel of equities for the equity fund permitted under the Act. Unit trusts have already proved useful in a similar way for small trust funds and they represent a genuine service to saving.

In the first edition of this book, I stated that in my view there was no doubt whatsoever that the unit trust movement had come to stay and that it is a most responsible movement. The last ten years have abundantly proved this statement. The figures alone on page 87 speak for themselves. The security aspect is quite first class. On the whole, unit trust charges are slightly more than those of investment trusts. While some unit trusts have been very successful they have not had the same remarkable success as investment trusts; in fact, in the nature of things, date of commencement, ready realizability of the units in times of difficulty, etc., it has been virtually impossible for them to do as well.

Unit trusts are probably more suitable to the small investor than investment trusts as there is always a ready market for the purchase or sale of unit trust units. They can be purchased in amounts of a few pounds; some trusts operate savings accounts for eventual purchase of units in which amounts as little as 25p can be deposited, and likewise the half-yearly distribution can be accumulated in the purchase of further units. This periodic purchase of units by small savings is a much bigger factor than many think. I understand there are over 100,000 accounts with an annual growth of £8 million and the rate is increasing.

As mentioned, the underlying securities of unit trusts are firmly in the hands of first class trust corporations; thus the security is absolutely first class.

On 13th October, 1959, the Association of Unit Trust Managers was formed of which most trusts, but unfortunately not all, are members. One of the objects of the Association is to agree standards of unit trust practice for the protection of the interests of the unit holders and to maintain the good name of the unit trust movement. This Association submitted a memorandum of evidence to the Jenkins Company Law Committee; clearly the Association was not satisfied with the present position and urged that legislation should be codified in a separate enactment. The Association rightly pointed out that the unit trust movement is a healthy, virile and reputable movement. In its view the present methods are unduly cumbersome, and its recommendations to the Jenkins Company Law Committee included the following:

(a) That legislation relating to unit trusts should be codified in a separate enactment to be called the Unit Trusts Act. (I sympathize with the Association's obvious desire to get away from the indignity of receiving its regulations by way of the Prevention of Fraud (Investments) Act, 1958 – it is quite undeserved.)
(b) That this Act should contain a specimen form of trust deed and any unit trust should be deemed to be constituted under this specimen form except to the extent that the document constituting the trust sets out alterations or additions.
(c) That this Act should set out specifically the present scheduled matters and the Board's regulations, should take into account the Association's own recommendations, and should embody any other matters which the Jenkins Committee considers should be incorporated, but should not attempt to establish minute control over the day-to-day operations of managers.

I think that the movement has proved its worth and has demonstrated its sense of responsibility. It should now be treated as an adult and not tied so tightly to the apron-strings of the D.T.I.

The Jenkins Committee in its report supported the unit trust movement and made a number of recommendations of a helpful nature, but so far nothing has been done or appears to be contemplated in the new Companies Act to implement its recommendations. Whatever else happens to liberalize the unit trust movement I feel strongly that the trustee must continue to be a first class large institution, such as one of the big insurance companies or the joint stock banks.

PART 3

# Corporation Tax and Capital Gains Tax and their effect

PART 3

# Corporation Tax and Capital Gains Tax

*Introduction*

It is essential that any book on investments should make some reference to Corporation Tax and Capital Gains Tax, particularly as these taxes are relatively new factors in the art and practice of investment, and both have been amended recently.

*Corporation Tax*

Obviously, it is not possible in a few paragraphs even to epitomize the scope of the new tax, because companies in their operation vary so greatly. And this is an investment book, not a book on taxation.

Corporation Tax commenced on 6th April, 1965. It applies to all companies but not to individuals; the latter are subject to whatever income tax is appropriate to their incomes. Charities and pension funds (in general terms) are not liable to tax.

Up to 6th April, 1965, companies paid income tax on their profits for tax purposes, plus, sometimes, a profits tax, also calculated on profits. Companies paid a total of approximately 55 per cent. in tax but profits distributed as dividends were franked for income tax; thus the dividend cost to the company was only the net amount after income tax.

Under the Corporation Tax system operating until 5th April, 1973, companies paid a flat rate of tax on profits (this varied between 40 and 45 per cent., with a special rate of 37½ per cent. for life assurance companies), and, in paying dividends, deducted income tax, acting as collectors for the Inland Revenue, to whom they accounted for the tax so deducted. The cost to the company of the dividend was thus the gross amount, except in the case of investment income that had suffered income tax, as the income tax deducted could be offset.

The introduction of Corporation Tax made a marked change in the method of raising new capital by public companies. Before 1965, the favourite medium was rights issues of ordinary shares; as with high interest rates, raising money on loan capital was a good deal more expensive than on a rights issue of ordinary shares.

With Corporation Tax, the interest on loan capital is a charge before arriving at the Corporation Tax liability. With a 40 per cent. Corporation Tax, a 10 per cent. debenture coupon costs the company only 6 per cent., whereas a rights issue costs the gross yield based on the issue price. Neither must it be overlooked that an issue of a debenture or an unsecured loan stock is valuable in gearing up the equity capital. Everything in excess of the 6 per cent. referred to, which the company earns from investing the proceeds of the loan capital issue, belongs to the equity shareholders. It's rather like buying a house under mortgage; the building society gets a flat rate of interest subject to some of the ups and downs of interest rates in general, and the borrower gets the extra value which inflation adds to the value of the house. But high gearing is dangerous for companies which are vulnerable to peak and trough profits as the lower the profits the much higher the percentage taken by the fixed interest capital before the equity shareholder comes in.

The following figures show the remarkable result of the 1965 change in taxation on the new issue market. The 1966 figure for ordinary shares is misleading as it included £60 million for British Petroleum which had a special tax position.

NEW CAPITAL ISSUES IN THE UNITED KINGDOM

*£ millions*

| | *1962* | *1963* | *1964* | *1965* | *1966* |
|---|---|---|---|---|---|
| Debenture and Loan Stocks: | | | | | |
| Convertible .. .. .. | 41·0 | 35·3 | 60·2 | 28·1 | 38·2 |
| Non-Convertible .. .. | 132·8 | 236·2 | 173·8 | 426·5 | 432·6 |
| Preference .. .. .. .. | 5·3 | 14·7 | 10·7 | 3·2 | 14·6 |
| Ordinary .. .. .. .. | 233·9 | 163·9 | 168·9 | 45·5 | 136·8 |
| | 413·0 | 450·1 | 413·6 | 503·3 | 622·2 |

There is no need to work out ratios to grasp the point. Mark you, this cannot go on forever because there must come a time when the institutions who largely provide the money become stuffed with debentures and loan issues, and they want some more equity capital. In fact, if inflation continues unabated, I foresee the time when the institutions will demand that the interest and capital of debentures and other fixed-interest capital are geared to the cost of living. As mentioned elsewhere in this book there was one small issue in 1965 which did precisely this. It was termed an 8 per cent. Cost of Living Stock (Unsecured) and it provided for a seven-year review of both the interest rate and the redemption price of the stock by reference to any rise in the cost of living as evidenced by the official Index of Retail Prices – a formula which could result in a maximum rate of interest of 10 per cent. and a maximum maturity price of £125 per cent.

However, the need has so far been met by the convertible stock. Indeed, the late sixties to early seventies have seen considerable growth of convertible debentures and unsecured loan stocks, also the latter with warrants attached. In this way options to convert into or to take up equities provide the prospect of capital growth while in the meantime high interest yields are obtained on the convertible debentures and loan stocks.

On the conversion of the convertible stock or the exercise of the warrants more ordinary shares are obviously created, but from the issuing company's point of view the evil day is, at least, postponed.

*The Imputation System of Corporation Tax*

As from 6th April, 1973, the existing system of Corporation Tax was replaced by a new system, called Imputation. The reasons for the change were to bring the U.K. system more in line with Continental practice following our entry into the E.E.C. and to encourage the distribution of dividends at the expense of retentions – particularly ironical as the introduction of the new system coincided with a period of dividend restraint.

The basic point about the new system is that the amount of Corporation Tax paid varies according to the proportion of profits distributed in the form of dividends. What happens is that dividends are now declared and paid net of Advance Corporation Tax (A.C.T.) and the A.C.T. reduces the company's Main Corporation Tax charge. The rate of A.C.T. for 1973–74 is 30 per cent., which happily corresponds with the basic rate of income tax. The shareholder receives his dividends net and gets a tax credit in respect of the A.C.T. deducted. The investor not liable to income tax gets the 'tax deducted in paying the dividend' refunded by producing the A.C.T. certificate to his Inspector of Taxes. There is no compulsion for the rate of A.C.T. to equal the basic rate of income tax, but obviously it is very convenient from the point of view of simplicity.

The rate of Main Corporation Tax for 1973–74 has not yet been finally fixed, but it has been widely assumed that it will be 50 per cent. and this assumption is made in the following examples.

What then are the effects of the new system? It is probably best illustrated by examining the situation for a typical company, whose profits are earned wholly in the U.K. Assume that pre-tax profits are £100,000, then the situation under the old system, with Corporation Tax at 40 per cent., was:

| | *All profits distributed* | *All profits retained* |
|---|---|---|
| | £ | £ |
| Pre-tax profits .. .. .. .. | 100,000 | 100,000 |
| Corporation tax at 40% .. .. .. | 40,000 | 40,000 |
| | 60,000 | 60,000 |
| Gross dividend .. .. .. .. | 60,000 | *nil* |
| Retention .. .. .. .. .. | *nil* | 60,000 |

Under the new system the situation becomes:

| | *All profits distributed* | *All profits retained* |
|---|---|---|
| | £ | £ |
| Pre-tax profits .. .. .. .. | 100,000 | 100,000 |
| Corporation tax at 50% .. .. .. | 50,000 | 50,000 |
| | 50,000 | 50,000 |
| Dividend .. .. .. .. .. | 50,000 net | *nil* |
| Retention .. .. .. .. .. | *nil* | 50,000 |
| The gross dividend* is .. .. .. | 71,429 | |
| | = 50,000 | |
| A.C.T.* .. .. .. .. .. | 21,429 net | |
| | 71,429 gross | |
| Total corporation tax liability .. .. | 28,571 | 50,000 |

* The gross dividend is the net dividend grossed for tax at 30 per cent. and the difference between the gross and net dividends is A.C.T.

From these examples it will be seen that under the new system the maximum distribution rises from £60,000 to £71,429, i.e. by just over 19 per cent., while with a nil distribution the amount retained falls from £60,000 to £50,000, i.e. by 16⅔ per cent. Thus under the new system a company which distributes a high proportion of its profits in the form of dividends pays a lower overall rate of Corporation Tax, after allowing for the A.C.T. credit, than a company which retains a higher proportion of its profits because in the latter case the A.C.T. credit will be less.

Clearly to obtain the maximum advantage from the new system a company must distribute as much of its profits as possible. It will thus be of advantage to companies including investment trusts where the dividend cover under the old system was low. Investment trusts will also benefit from higher payouts from companies in which they have holdings. It will be disadvantageous to companies wishing to retain a higher proportion of profits to finance expansion. However, with dividend restraint, under the Government's prices and incomes policy, most companies cannot yet obtain the maximum advantage from the new system.

*Price/Earnings Ratio as Originally Introduced*

Corporation Tax resulted in more emphasis being placed upon the price/earnings ratio, namely the number of times by which the price exceeds the earnings per share. Personally I prefer to look at the dividend yield and the earnings yield. It is true that the price/earnings ratio is used internationally but in view of the taxation differences between the various nations I could not see it as a standard yardstick of value.

What does the price/earnings ratio of itself tell the investor? I suggest that of itself it tells the investor very little. A high price/earnings ratio could mean a vigorous growth share or the share of a company doing very badly and making little profit. Similarly a low price/earnings ratio could indicate a share of a company with a long record of stagnation or the share of a good company which is undervalued.

Under the pre-1973 system of Corporation Tax, earnings were simply defined as profits after tax, which was also the maximum amount available for distribution to shareholders. The dividend cover was simply the number of times net earnings exceeded the gross dividends paid, while the price/earnings ratio was the number of times the price of the share exceeded the earnings attributed to that share.

Under the new system the position is, unfortunately, far from straightforward, as the earnings vary according to the proportion of profits distributed.

In calculating the P/E ratio, therefore, at least two assumptions may be made: either that earnings are equal to the maximum gross dividends payable – the full distribution basis – or that earnings are the maximum amount that can be retained – the nil distribution basis.

In the example (p. 102) earnings under the full distribution basis are £71,429 and under the nil distribution basis £50,000. Under the old system earnings under both assumptions were £60,000. Thus according to your choice of definition, earnings rise by 19 per cent. or fall by 16⅔ per cent. under the new system. Conversely, price/earnings ratios fall by 16 per cent. under the maximum distribution basis or rise by 20 per cent. under the nil distribution basis. The situation is even more complicated if the company has large overseas earnings, in which case it may not pay sufficient Corporation Tax to offset fully the A.C.T. paid on dividends. A third definition, called the net basis, has therefore been devised, which is similar to the nil basis except that the company's tax charge contains any unrelieved A.C.T. arising from a dividend payment from overseas earnings. Unless the company does have significant overseas earnings the result is the same under the nil and net basis.

To calculate dividend cover the full distribution basis should be used to find earnings as this corresponds with the maximum amount that can be distributed without uncovering the dividend; the cover is thus still the number of times by which the dividend exceeds earnings per share.

The calculation of P/E ratios under the new system has given rise to considerable confusion and this has not been helped by the fact that there is no clear agreement between such bodies as the Society of Investment Analysts, the Institute of Chartered Accountants, the financial press and the statistical services as to which method should be adopted.

The situation is thus far from clear for investors, who can be forgiven for going back to dividend yield as a means of assessing the relative attractiveness of a share. Nevertheless, it is to be hoped that agreement will be soon reached on a universal measurement.

What is certain is that the new-style P/E ratio, however it is calculated, will, it seems to me, never be as good a comparative measurement as the old P/E ratio was.

However, as with every other change, once investors have got used to thinking in any new agreed terms it does not matter that they are not strictly comparable with the old ones.

*The End of the Net U.K. Rate*

As I have already stated, I regard the end of the net U.K. rate as a blessing in disguise. It was a great worry to pension fund managers and to all those not liable to income tax on their incomes, or not liable at the full standard rate of tax. All such investors had the job of reclaiming income tax which had been deducted at source and each reclaim was limited to the net U.K. rate.

As previously mentioned some companies, the oil companies for example, had notoriously low net U.K. rates – in fact, more often than not they paid no U.K. tax at all, their tax, owing to reciprocal arrangements, being franked by overseas taxation. Then there were cases like Babcock & Wilcox and the P. & O. where dividends on occasions suddenly went from net U.K. rates reasonably near to the U.K. standard rate of tax to very low net U.K. rates. 'The net U.K. rate company', as I mentioned earlier, was hardest hit by the change in Corporation Tax but an overspill arrangement assisted them to a varying extent in the change-over. But it will be a comfort to know that for funds and individuals not subject to tax, the complications of the net U.K. rate has disappeared. Inspectors of Taxes will also heave a sigh of relief, as it will take much of the sting out of income tax repayment claim work.

*Tax Agreement with the United States*

The tax agreement with the United States substituted a withholding tax of 15 per cent. for income tax on British dividends payable to U.S. residents and maintains the U.S. rate at 15 per cent. This will have to be varied following our new tax structure.

*Capital Gains Tax*

Here again I must warn that in the space available I can only comment on this tax in broad outline. It is immensely complicated and pages upon pages of print are used up in explaining its scope and incidence. The paper work in its administration is enormous.

Up to 6th April, 1965, there was a short-term Capital Gains Tax in respect of profits less losses incurred within six months, chargeable at the investor's top rate of tax. From 6th April, 1965, the short term capital gains tax period was increased to twelve months and a long-term capital gains tax set up of 30 per cent. on all other gains for individuals, including evaluated gains (exceeding £5,000) on the death of the investor. For annual gains of less than

£5,000, the investor could and still can pay at his top rate of tax on half the long-term gains.

The basis for calculating capital gains is the actual cost at the time of the acquisition of the investment, or, if held before 6th April, 1965, the alternative of the value on that date and cost, whichever best suits the investor. The Exchange Telegraph Company has published a book, giving the prices as at 6th April, 1965, for all quoted investments after allowing for scrip, rights issues, etc.

The basis for losses is the cost at the time of acquisition but if acquired before 6th April, 1965, the value at that date will apply but only if it produces a smaller loss.

Losses can only be set off against profits or carried forward against future profits. In other words, you cannot recover any loss unless you have equivalent gains to set against it.

Broadly, companies pay at the Corporation Tax rate, as gains less losses form part of their profits. There are some concessions; no gains tax is payable for instance on the replacement of assets for like assets.

Since 1965, there have been considerable changes in the tax. Short-term gains tax has been abolished and all gains are now classed as one. Significant concessions have been introduced for investment and unit trusts and for dealings in them (see above). Capital Gains Tax on death has been abolished and gilt-edged stocks are now entirely free from Capital Gains Tax if held for more than one year – although still subject to tax if held for less.

These changes have tended to ease the burden of the tax but have not changed its basic effect, which is to make investment less profitable, or rendered it much less complicated or time consuming.

To me, the most unpleasant aspects of the tax are: (a) the extra work it involves – the paper work is enormous; (b) the difficulty of judging whether an exchange from one investment to another justifies the handicap of the gains tax payable; and (c) the sluggish effect that the tax, by inhibiting market operations, has upon the market.

I feel that eventually we shall learn to live with the Capital Gains Tax, but in the meantime many a justified exchange will not take place because the investor will only see in the operation a certain liability for capital gains which he will have to pay in the near future.

If he acts, there is £*x* to pay the Inland Revenue. If he does nothing, nothing to pay the Revenue. But past experience has time and time again shown that some shares become over-valued. Look back over ten years and consider the highs of insurance shares, property shares, the computer shares. Had the present type of Capital Gains Tax been in operation on 6th April, 1961, and the current timid action of investors an inert force to deal with, then the majority of investors would have stuck to these over-valued shares rather than face a temporary reduction in the market value of their portfolios due to a heavy capital gains payment.

Let us take an example based on fact and make the assumption that Capital Gains Tax in its present form came into force on 6th April, 1961. In mid-1961 let us suppose an investor on his investment consultant's advice sold his holding of 2,000 Commercial Union shares at £3·50 after expenses – a month or two earlier they had reached over £4·00. Assuming the price for Capital Gains was £2·10, the capital gains assessment would be £1·40 per share on 2,000 shares, namely £2,800 at 30 per cent. = £840. Supposing the proceeds of £6,160 after reserving for Capital Gains Tax were invested in the Alliance Trust at the equivalent of £1·20 after expenses and adjustments for scrip issues as could have been done at the time. Many transactions of this type were done in 1961 and 1962. Many other investors stayed with their insurance shares, but the current positions of the two classes of investor would today be very different.

The investor who did nothing would have 4,000 Commercial Union shares worth at the present price of £2·40, £6,720, while the investor who exchanged into Alliance Trust shares would, even after deducting the hypothetical Capital Gains Tax, have 5,130 Alliance Trust shares (present price £1·84), now worth £9,439, considerably more than his purchase price of £6,160. So, even assuming he paid Capital Gains Tax, he would be better off by £2,719.

I cannot stress too strongly that an immediate payment of Capital Gains Tax should not put off what seems to be the right investment decision. The right judgement will still be worth its weight in gold.

There is much talk of offsetting capital profits against capital losses. With a first class portfolio which has already been cleaned up, the chance of capital losses due to cleaning up will be rare. There may be a number of shares standing below the basic price for capital gains, but why throw away 70 per cent. of the potential recovery to book value to secure 30 per cent. of it, particularly if you have faith that the share will eventually recover in price? In my view, the recovery prospects of a good share must be dim before an offsetting capital gains loss is justified. First, there must be a stock to exchange into which has almost certainly greater recovery prospects.

If you mistime a purchase of a British Government Stock, sell it within the year into a similar stock and set up a capital gains loss, for use against future profits.

*'G' Plan*

Under this plan, certain overseas investors were able to have their dividends on most British equities paid gross, i.e. without income tax being deducted, but this plan has been temporarily suspended following the changes in the taxation system. Doubtless a similar scheme will be introduced in due course.

# PART 4

# The Art Applied

CHAPTER 13

# Personal and Family Trusts

*The Nature and Variety of these Trusts*

This is the group of trusts created by individuals under wills or by settlements, in favour of other individuals. In the majority of cases the trusts will be in favour of wife or husband and the issue of the marriage, but other beneficiaries may include grandchildren, nephews, nieces; the scope is wide.

Under a family trust a man may provide for his wife to receive the income from the settled capital during her life and, subject to avoiding the 'rule against perpetuities', a further life interest, upon her death, to his children, with reversion to his grandchildren. Such a trust could last for a period of over sixty years – indeed, even a hundred years. If the life interests are limited to the wife or husband, the trust will be of more modest duration, although a marriage settlement with life interest to surviving spouse will often last for sixty years.

Thus we at once note that the duration of a personal trust cannot be ascertained with any certainty, but that it may be lengthy.

A professional trustee will have a large variety of personal trusts under its care and, although the majority will in essentials follow the family trust pattern, there will be those cases where there is no issue of the marriage and other beneficiaries will be provided for. Trusts give play for the individual idiosyncrasies of the testator or settlor. There will be gifts-over to charities, the protective-trust provisions for the son who is not 'good' with money and the daughter who has made an unpopular marriage: trusts for the backward child. Grandfather or grandmother will make provision in trust to enable grandson or granddaughter to go to a public school; there will even be similar trusts which an uncle will make in favour of his favourite niece or nephew. Fathers, partly to divorce income from their own income for tax purposes, will create accumulative trusts in favour of their infant children. There will be the trusts which the family does not speak about; the trusts in favour of the settlor's favourite charity; the settlor may even set up his own charity.

*The Diverse Factors*

It will have been noted that the types and objects of these trusts vary considerably. There are other variants.

Estate duty is leviable when the capital of a personal trust passes from one beneficiary to another, and, what is more, for the purpose of ascertaining the rate of duty all assets including gifts (see below) made by him within seven years of his death less liabilities passing on the death of the beneficiary are aggregable with the trust funds passing. There is an exception: no estate duty is payable on a fund in which the surviving spouse had a life interest if the fund has already borne duty on the death of the other spouse.

It will be noted that not only has the trustee of a personal trust a trust of unknown duration, but he may also have to meet at any time an unknown liability for estate duty. A trust of long duration is the discretionary family trust where the purpose of the trust is to avoid, for estate duty purposes, a passing of the capital from one beneficiary to another, thus obviating claims for death duties when individual members of the discretionary group die.

The trustee of a personal trust must ascertain his investment powers and stick to them rigidly. His investment powers should be set out in the deed or will which creates the trust. Some of the investment clauses included in deeds in the early part of the century are long and tortuously worded; they include investments which have ceased to exist, and the draftsmen in their efforts to cover the field fully have been verbose and the result is not readily discernible. This type of clause in the end gives the trustee something less than full powers of investment. In recent years it has become the practice to give trustees, particularly trust corporations, full power to invest the trust funds as if they were the personal property of the trustees. This is a sensible provision.

If the deed or will creating the trust omits to state any investment powers, then the trustee is limited to the investments prescribed in the Trustee Investments Act, 1961, which came into force on the 4th August, 1961. The terms of this Act are set out on pages 147 to 154. Previously the statutory powers of investments were prescribed by the Trustee Act, 1925 – namely, a limited number of fixed-interest securities plus Bank of Ireland stock.

A trustee of a personal trust has always to remember that he is acting for two distinct classes of beneficiary – the life tenant, who for his part is only interested (and I use the words literally) in increasing income payments, and the remainderman, who desires the largest possible sum of money to come to him when the life tenant has ceased to exist.

These two interests are often referred to as 'conflicting interests', as indeed they can be. It would be quite improper, for example, to invest a large proportion of the fund in low-coupon dated stocks standing at a substantial discount, as this unduly favours the remainderman. It would be equally inappropriate to invest a large proportion of the fund in high-coupon dated stocks standing at a substantial premium, as this unduly favours the life tenant. I would suggest that if it was desirable for an investment to be made in a low-coupon dated stock at a discount then it would be reasonable, with a view to maintaining the life tenant's income, to match the low-coupon stock with a high-coupon stock of a similar date even if standing at a premium.

Having said all this I should mention that one way of ensuring the income, is to protect the capital; speculative investments may give a high return for a short period, but what the life tenant wants is a steady income which never decreases but, on the contrary, increases.

*Varying Circumstances of Life Tenant*

The trustee, if he is to do his job properly, must know something about the individual circumstances of the life tenant, including such matters as:

(a) the age of the life tenant;
(b) whether married, a widow or widower, or single;
(c) his or her financial circumstances apart from the trust;
(d) his or her financial responsibilities;
(e) the approximate tax rate, which is important and can be deduced from (c). If the life tenant pays income tax of 90 per cent. on the top slice of his income there is usually little point in buying a high yielding stock or share. Capital appreciation even if subject to capital gains tax would doubtless be preferred if the remaindermen were members of his family, but if he is not interested in the remaindermen he may prefer a current yield of 8 per cent. gross to a yield of 3½ per cent. gross, since he can always covenant away his surplus income to friends.

9

He pays the covenant less the basic rate of tax which the beneficiary may reclaim in whole or part. But the settlor cannot secure relief on the covenant at the higher tax rates. If, on the other hand, the life tenant is *not* liable to tax at the basic rate, high yielding shares and stocks would be more suitable;

(f) the residence. If the life tenant is resident overseas, then, for fixed-interest stocks, the trustees might want to concentrate on those British government stocks which are not subject to tax in the hands of non-residents (see page 25).

Lastly, in those cases where a trustee is appointed jointly with other trustees, he will have to consult with those trustees.

To sum up, a trustee who acts for a variety of personal trusts has to keep in mind:

(i) that the objects of each trust will vary tremendously;
(ii) that the majority of trusts will be for an unknown period;
(iii) that there will be liabilities for estate duty for unknown amounts payable at a time which can only be roughly estimated;
(iv) that the investment powers will vary from trust to trust;
(v) that the respective interests of the life tenants and remaindermen will have to be watched;
(vi) that he will have to take into account the individual circumstances of the beneficiaries;
(vii) that where there is a joint trustee his approval has to be secured.

*The Investment of the Funds of a Personal Trust*

Having obtained all the necessary information concerning the beneficiary and the trust, the trustee must now consider how to invest the fund. Let us assume that the trust is established with a sum of money and that the trust deed gives the trustee full powers of investment.

The first problem, therefore, is to consider how much, if any, of the fund should be invested in fixed-interest stocks and how much in equities. I am going to state at once that I feel that, wherever there are liabilities at some time to be provided for, then a certain proportion of the fund should be invested in fixed-interest securities. There is no hard and fast rule as to what the proportion should be.

The Trustee Investments Act gives us a clue when in effect it stipulates that a fund subject to statutory powers of investment shall have at least 50 per cent. in fixed-interest securities when the fund is set up. In our example, however, we are dealing with a trust which has full powers of investment. In deciding the proportions the trustee must bear in mind the relative market situation of fixed-interest securities and equities. When the economy of the country is obviously flourishing, more could go into equities and, alternatively, when trade prospects are uncertain or bad, more could be put into fixed-interest stocks.

There are times when equities look over-valued and there are times when fixed interest appears to be over-valued – an obvious example of the latter was the Dalton period of low interest rates. The percentages in fixed interest and equities will be adjusted according to circumstances. A decision such as this can be taken only after considerable thought and applied skill, and, as it is an exercise in foresight and not hindsight, it is subject to error.

*Setting up the Fund*

Let us go through the exercise of setting up the fund which has full powers of investment and for the purpose let us choose a fund of £100,000 cash. Although in this trust the trustee has full powers of investment, we will choose a distribution of 30 per cent. in fixed

| | | | | *Redemption yields* | |
|---|---|---|---|---|---|
| | | | | *Gross to* | |
| | | *Price* | *Flat yield* | *final date* | *Net*[1] |
| £ | | £ | £ | £ | £ |
| 1,000 | Building Society Deposit (6·25% net)[2] | — | 8·93 | — | — |
| 9,000 | equally between: | | | | |
| | Savings 3% 1965–75 | 89½ | 3·35 | 8·73 | 7·79 |
| | Electricity 3% 1974–77 | 83¼ | 3·60 | 8·45 | 7·33 |
| | Treasury 3% 1979 | 73 | 4·18 | 9·09 | 7·91 |
| | Treasury 3½% 1977–80 | 69¾ | 5·05 | 9·72 | 8·39 |
| | Treasury 3½% 1979–81 | 67½ | 5·17 | 9·64 | 8·32 |
| 2,500 | Treasury 9% Convertible 1980[3] | 91¾ | 9·72 | 10·60 | 7·81 |
| 2,500 | Treasury 9½% 1999 | 86¾ | 11·00 | 11·12 | 7·89 |
| 15,000 | in a selection of first-class long-dated debenture and loan stocks. Average yield £11·5% | | | | |
| £30,000 | Average yield on the £30,000 invested: £8·57% | | | | |

[1] After income tax at 30 per cent.

[2] Share a/c 6·75 per cent. equivalent gross 9·64 per cent. liable to tax in the hands of high rate payers on the basis of (the rate — 30) per cent.

[3] Redeemable at par in March 1980 or, at the option of the holder, convertible into 9% Conversion Stock 2,000 on basis of £110 of this stock for every £100 of Treasury 9% Convertible held.

interest and 70 per cent. in equities. We have chosen these proportions because we feel, at the time of the investment, the equity market is reasonably stable and the future is not unduly discounted; moreover, fixed-interest stocks appear to be reasonably valued.

*Fixed-interest Stocks* – Bearing in mind what has been written on pages 17 to 34 concerning fixed-interest securities, the trustee has to select fixed-interest securities to a total of £30,000. Thirty per cent. is a modest proportion, so I would suggest that he keeps to redeemable stocks. My selection would be as shown in table on page 115.

The building society deposit will be useful in providing the necessary cash to take up rights as they are offered on any of the equities selected. This deposit and the £9,000 in medium shorts, represent the trust's sheet-anchor. The other £20,000 is invested in long-dated stocks, taking the view that interest rates are high at the present time. The £30,000 in fixed-interest stocks would give a current yield of £8·57 per cent. If, after taking all the facts into consideration, growth is deemed more important than yield, the trustee could double the participation in short medium stocks and for the balance of the £30,000 buy low-coupon medium to long-dated British government and debenture stocks which are standing well below par.

*Equities* – Now as regards the 70 per cent. that it is proposed to put into equities; the problems of equity investment have been considered on pages 35 to 69. It is just a case of spreading the £70,000 over industry, omitting those sections whose future is at present especially obscure. I would suggest an investment of £2,000–£2,500 each in the giant companies and £1,000–£1,500 each in the followers.

The aim is a balanced portfolio. It could be argued that this could be achieved by simply buying investment trusts. The professional trustee would, however, hope to pick shares which are going to perform better than the very wide spread of an investment trust portfolio; in any case, the trustee requires liquidity which goes with market leaders, and needs a little more yield than can be secured from investment trust equities.

Appendix 1 lists some 150 equities from which to choose and in making our choice we will have regard to diversification of interests and as to whether the current price is reasonable – bearing in mind all known facts. Here our stockbroker's views should be carefully considered. The selection would, however, probably consist of some

| | | | | | |
|---|---|---|---|---|---|
| 12 | equities of | £2,500 | each | = | £30,000 |
| 11 | ,, ,, | £2,000 | ,, | = | £22,000 |
| 12 | ,, ,, | £1,500 | ,, | = | £18,000 |
| 35 | | | | | £70,000 |

In selecting the shares, well-known growth shares will be combined with some higher yielding equities and the all-over yield on the equity fund would be in the neighbourhood of £4·50 per cent. The yield on the whole fund would thus be £5·72 per cent., made up as follows:

| | | *Average yield* % | *Gross income* |
|---|---|---|---|
| Fixed-interest fund | £30,000 .. | £8·57 | £2,571 |
| Equity fund | £70,000 .. | £4·50 | £3,150 |
| Average yield £5·72% | | | £5,721 |

If this trust were being set up as a result of a will and the deceased's wife had a life interest, then there would be no *estate duty* problems on her death; but, if the fund had been settled in trust in the lifetime of the settlor in favour of his wife, then estate duty would arise. A £100,000 fund, even ignoring any other fund or assets which might have to be aggregated with it, would be subject to estate duty at an overall rate of 37·25 per cent. and, if the life tenant were to die within a few years of the setting-up of the trust, the trustee might well wish that he had invested more money in fixed-interest securities. Estate duty would also arise on the settlor's death (except in the case of a marriage settlement) if he did not survive the date of the settlement by seven years, and the duty would be chargeable against the fund. There is, however, marginal relief as follows: death in fifth year, 85 per cent. of the duty is payable; in sixth year, 70 per cent.; in seventh year, 40 per cent. If death occurs within first four years the full duty is payable. Gifts to charities are free of estate duty if death occurs after twelve months from time of giving.

I have assumed above that the trust fund starts with a cash sum of £100,000, but it might well be otherwise. Supposing a deceased has left a higgledy-piggledy list of investments. The executor's first task is to effect sales to provide estate duty, and he will use this as an opportunity to weed out inferior securities. It is a fact that most investors hang on to their poor stuff only to disgorge it on death. A review of the investments in conjunction with the trust's stockbrokers is desirable before deciding on the sales. This can be done at the same time as the investments are valued for probate. Here I would stress the need to obtain probate quickly, as good delivery of investments cannot be given until probate is obtained and the executors are registered on the books of the companies concerned. Under the latest Finance Act probate value is the lower of the value at date of death and the realization proceeds of an investment, provided it is sold or realized within one year from the date of death.

Having provided enough to meet the estate duty liability, the trustee must then have another look at the fund. Taking all the factors into consideration, he will have to decide the appropriate proportions of fixed-interest and equities respectively, and whether some of the holdings are excessive in amount and whether others are unsuitable. As regards the latter I recommend ruthlessness.

In my experience I have found it is almost invariably wrong to hang on to inferior high yielding securities. Certain shares, namely mining, rubber and tea shares, should be left to the experts engaged in the industry and not included in a normal trust portfolio. They are not the type of investment to appear in a portfolio designed to give a widow a stable income. The trustee will never again have an opportunity like this to clean up the fund, but if he allows inferior investments with high yields to stay in the portfolio he will have to meet the criticism of the life tenant when later he sells them and reduces the income, because it might take a year or two before the company concerned, often through no fault of his own, runs into trouble and reduces its dividend. It should be mentioned that, unless the life tenant is a trustee or under the terms of the will must be consulted on investments, the life tenant's criticism has no validity, but the trustee will wish to avoid if possible having 'to live' with a disgruntled beneficiary.

Some testators, while limiting the trusts set up under their wills to the statutory powers of investment, authorize the trustees to retain any investments held by them at the time of their death. This provision is not without its problems. The trustee is under temptation to retain inferior equities to bolster up yield, while an outstandingly successful equity will, after the lapse of years, have a value quite out of proportion to the total value of the fund and, because of its growth, have an exceedingly low current yield. The trustee cannot reduce the holding and invest the whole of the proceeds in equities. However, the Trustee Investments Act does allow a trustee to keep 'retained' investments in a separate fund and to apply the 50/50 rule to the balance. But the proceeds of the sale of any 'retained' investment accrue 50/50 to the two statutory funds – thus only half the proceeds of the sale of 'retained' investments can be invested in equities.

*Records and Reviews* – The trustee, having set up what he hopes will prove to be a satisfactory fund, cannot go to sleep or ease up. Adequate records must be set up and kept up to date and be readily available. The trust fund must be reviewed in conjunction with the trust's stockbrokers at least once a year and possibly twice. A professional trustee such as a trust corporation will be reviewing individual trust funds every working day. As a result of these reviews certain decisions will be taken. If, for example, a decision is made to sell a particular share, it can be sold, if appropriate, on all trusts. Thus, although each individual trust fund will go through the operation of a review perhaps only once in a year, the trust investments will actually be under constant review by reason of the constant reviewing of other trusts.

One word of warning: if a trustee buys an unauthorized investment he is responsible for any loss occasioned thereby. If, for example, he bought six investments and they were all unauthorized, and out of five the trust fund made very substantial profits but incurred a loss on the other, the trustee would be liable to make good that loss without taking into account the profits on the other five investments.

CHAPTER 14

# Pension and Superannuation Funds

*Generally*

A pension fund trust is a very different type of trust from a personal trust. For a start, the fund may not be subject to any income tax (see page 124). Pension funds are governed by the 1921 Finance Act, where it was laid down that approved pension funds should be free from tax and the pensions themselves taxable. In the case of a pension fund there is no need to differentiate between capital and income as the same group of people, the pensioners and the prospective pensioners, is entitled to share in the fund. The normal year-to-year changes in the value of the fund, due to appreciation or depreciation, are not important. Unlike the life fund of an assurance company, pension funds are not under any legal obligation to show that the fund is solvent, taking into account market values.

When the fund is set up an actuary advises on the contributions necessary to provide the proposed scale of pensions. The rate of interest chosen (the basic rate) is the important factor; to give an example, with 2½ per cent. compound interest a sum of £1,000 per annum will amount to approximately £69,000 at the end of forty years, whereas with interest at 4½ per cent. the same sum will amount to approximately £112,000 at the end of forty years and to £164,000 at 6 per cent. I am informed that at the present time the rate used more often than not in calculation of contributions and benefits is 6½ per cent. compound interest. With older funds the rate could be as low as 4 per cent. Lower rates, all other things being equal, will provide larger surpluses on a valuation. Thus there would be proportionately greater sums to augment pensions and other benefits. One of the objects of the pension fund trustees will be to endeavour to invest the fund at a higher rate than the actuary provides for in his calculations. The majority of pension fund trustees have full powers of investment.

The very large majority of pension funds are growing and not diminishing. Most pension fund trustees have therefore no problems of having to realize securities at the right time or in difficult circumstances, because in the majority of the cases the contributions to the fund are more than adequate to meet pensions and the whole of the interest plus the balance of the contributions will be available for investing. Thus a pension fund is usually a continuous investor, which means there is a continuous averaging taking place – the trustees are buying whether the market is high or low but buying it is hoped, intelligently.

Pension fund trustees sometimes have opportunities for underwriting issues, and underwriting is usually a very profitable transaction. Underwriting profits can be taxable. The rule is that if the pension payments exceed the amount of the underwriting commissions received then the underwriting commission will not suffer tax.

Clearly, a pension fund which has been invested wisely over the year is likely to have a considerable appreciation on its equity stock holdings. There would be a case for writing up these holdings to some extent, using the profit built up in the books in this way for increasing pensions. Here we might note that a pension is a fixed-interest payment and if the portion of the pensioner's contributions put into equity stocks has kept pace with inflation there is a case for passing some of the appreciation to the pensioner.

*Investment Pattern and Spread*

In the early days of pension funds it was the practice to invest the whole fund, or a very large proportion of the fund, in fixed-interest securities. Those investment advisers who favoured equities have for many years been pressing pension fund trustees to invest an increasing proportion of their funds in equities, and in many cases the advice has been taken. Other trustees have from early days recognized the merits of equities.

The figures which are shown in the tables on page 122 obtained from the Radcliffe Committee report show the investment spread of pension funds in 1957.

The latest figures as supplied by the Central Statistical Office show that the emphasis on equities has continued. Pension funds are now putting at least 50 per cent. of their new monies in equities.

The annual rate of growth of all pension funds is estimated at more than £900 million.

The figures on page 123 show at the end of 1972 the pattern of investment for pension funds as a whole. Each trustee has to decide

## ASSETS OF MAIN SUPERANNUATION AND PENSION FUNDS 1957[1]

(Excluding funds reassured with insurance companies and local authority funds and covering about 90 per cent. of the remainder.)

| *Type of assets* | *Market value[2] of assets end 1957* £m. | % | *Net investment[3] during 1957* £m. | % |
|---|---|---|---|---|
| Gilt-edged | 570 | 34 | 40 | 20 |
| Overseas government, provincial and municipal securities | 54 | 3 | 2 | 1 |
| Securities of, and loans to, U.K. local authorities | 98 | 6 | 16 | 8 |
| Company debentures | 194 | 12 | 34 | 17 |
| Preference shares | 63 | 4 | 2 | 1 |
| Ordinary stocks and shares | 351 | 21 | 73 | 37 |
| Mortgages | 33 | 2 | 2 | 1 |
| Real property (excluding mortgages) | 42 | 3 | 10 | 5 |
| Life and annuity policies | 1 | — | 1 | 1 |
| Cash and other assets | 252 | 15 | 18 | 9 |
| Total assets | 1,658[2,4] | 100 | 198[3] | 100 |

[1] For accounting years ending between 1st April, 1957 and 31st March, 1958.

[2] Including £143 million assets valued at book values.

[3] Including £58 million net investment shown as the difference between the book value of the assets at the opening and closing balance sheet dates.

[4] Excluding local authority superannuation funds.

## ASSETS OF SUPERANNUATION FUNDS 1966

(Including private and local authority funds but excluding the main superannuation arrangements in the central government sector.)

| *Type of assets* | *Market value* £m. | % | *Net investment during 1966* £m. | % |
|---|---|---|---|---|
| Gilt-edged | 966 | 18 | 37 | 7 |
| U.K. local authority | 541 | 10 | 1 | — |
| Overseas government | 52 | 1 | −6 | −1 |
| Company debentures | 794 | 15 | 149 | 28 |
| Preference shares | 68 | 1 | −3 | −1 |
| Ordinary stocks and shares | 2,265 | 43 | 205 | 39 |
| Loans and mortgages | 294 | 5 | 86 | 16 |
| Cash and other assets | 402 | 7 | 62 | 12 |
| Total assets | 5,382 | 100 | 531 | 100 |

the pattern for his pension fund. The pattern will be maintained as further funds flow in for investment until conditions demand a change

ASSETS OF SUPERANNUATION FUNDS 1972

(Including private and local authority funds but excluding the main superannuation arrangements in the central government sector.)

| | *Market value* | | *Net investment during 1972* | |
|---|---|---|---|---|
| *Type of assets* | £m. | % | £m. | % |
| Gilt-edged | 1,303 | 12 | 18 | 2 |
| U.K. local authority | 377 | 3 | −18 | −2 |
| Overseas government | 30 | — | −4 | — |
| Company debentures | 1,222 | 11 | 14 | 1 |
| Preference shares | 36 | — | 3 | — |
| Ordinary stocks and shares | 6,434 | 57 | 549 | 57 |
| Loans and mortgages | 372 | 3 | 102 | 11 |
| Cash and other assets | 1,631 | 14 | 296 | 31 |
| Total assets | 11,405 | 100 | 960 | 100 |

in the pattern. In the figures set out above, net investment during 1957 clearly indicates a change in pattern compared with previous years, for, in 1957, 37 per cent. was invested in equities and 47 per cent. in fixed-interest stocks compared with 21 and 59 per cent. respectively of total pension funds. This clearly shows the trend in favour of equities. With 57 per cent. in equities in 1972, the trend has clearly continued.

There is at least one very large pension fund which is exclusively invested in equities. This fact has obviously pushed up the all-over percentage. At the time the first edition appeared in 1962 I wrote that there would appear to be further scope for pension funds increasing their participation in equity shares, particularly in view of the greater investment freedom now that many funds are no longer restricted to fixed-interest stocks by statute. The 1966 and 1972 figures show how true this prediction was. In normal equity markets I expect pension funds to invest more than half of their new monies in equities.

### *Setting up the Fund*

*Fixed-interest Stocks* – Consider the claims of fixed-interest stocks first; one must keep in mind that a pension fund is likely to be in operation for a very long time. The trustee could therefore with some advantage invest part of the fund in irredeemable stocks if they are chosen carefully and bought when interest rates are high. In other words, if a fund is set up on a 6 per cent. yield, and the trustee can get 10 per cent. or more on an irredeemable stock, he has left himself with a very satisfactory margin.

*Taxation*

The fully approved pension fund is not subject to income tax or to Capital Gains Tax.

It is the gross redemption yield which the pension trustee has to consider when he makes an investment. This yield should be calculated after taking into account any stamp duty and commission payable. Obviously, a pension fund trustee will endeavour to buy stocks which are not subject to stamp duty, and in buying debentures and other stocks which are normally subject to stamp duty he will try to buy them in scrip form. All pension fund trustees will endeavour to secure a fair quota of first class debentures. First class preference shares are very suitable for pension funds when interest rates are high, but not if they are overvalued compared with debenture stocks (see page 29). High interest rates make the pension trustee's life easier because he has no difficulty in bettering the basic interest rate of the pension fund. The trustee's task becomes worrying when he is forced to invest for more than a short period at a rate lower than the appropriate rate.

Long-term dated stocks are most suitable to a pension fund, but it would be inappropriate to buy such stocks if long-term rates were slipping, since there might be better opportunities of buying later. In such a case the trustee might 'go short' very temporarily. Here I mean this literally – a fund cannot afford to lose current income for long and the position must be watched daily. There will be occasions when short-term cash deposits will offer attractive yields – August 1973, for example, when 17 per cent. was obtained on seven-day call money – but the pension fund investment manager must not, in accepting the opportunities of very attractive short-term deposit rates, miss good opportunities for long-term investment. But subject to this the trustee should endeavour to have a fixed-interest section which has balance having regard to the classes of fixed-interest stock and to their maturity dates. He must avoid having too large a proportion of the fund in stocks redeemable about the same time in case at the time of repayment interest rates are low.

*Equities* – As in the purchase of fixed-interest stocks, the trustee will also in the case of equity stocks have regard to the considerations set out earlier in these pages. He must aim at spread and diversification. I would suggest that not more than ½ per cent. of the fund should be invested in one equity unless the equity is a first class giant, when the amount might be 1½ per cent.

Until the advent of Corporation Tax companies whose preference and ordinary shares had a low net U.K. rate (see page 105) were unattractive to pension funds. This meant that few pension funds invested in oil shares. However, Corporation Tax put an end to the net U.K. rate and investment managers can no longer fall into the trap of buying shares which suddenly acquire low net U.K. rates – Babcock and Wilcox and P. & O. have been examples of this. For the same reason investment trust shares were not then suitable to pension funds. The low net U.K. rates sprung from the fact that a large percentage of their funds were invested in North American securities.

With the end of the net U.K. rate, investment trust shares could prove very attractive to pension funds as this is an excellent way of participating in the assured growth of American common stocks without having to pay the dollar premium. Some investment trusts have 50 per cent. of their funds in American stocks (see page 82). The larger pension funds could take a direct interest in American common stocks, provided the dollar premium, which in recent months has been as high as 40 per cent. does not prohibit the exercise. A further disadvantage of direct participation in American common stocks is the 15 per cent. withholding tax which cannot be reclaimed by gross funds.

Although pension fund trustees should be ready to seek profitable investment in other parts of the world they might be prejudiced against the industrial shares of countries in Europe after the experience of the last fifty years or so and they must all the time bear in mind that currency risks and political risks are a factor with overseas investment.

The small pension fund could well seek its quota of equity investment through investment trusts or through the unit trusts which are tailored to meet their equity requirements. Earlier I have mentioned a large pension fund which is exclusively invested in equities. Personally, I feel that there is always scope for having a percentage of a pension fund in fixed-interest stocks; there is then room for manœuvre. I know of one pension fund, which is still growing rapidly, which is invested by admitted experts who not long ago worked on the following ratio: 40 per cent. British government, 35 per cent. debentures and 25 per cent. equities. Even experts differ.

My own preference is for 75 per cent. in equities and 25 per cent. in fixed-interest with a base of 50/50 when all the joy has gone out of the equity market. The simplest way of altering the percentages and taking advantage of market conditions is in the direction of new monies.

*Some Miscellaneous Points*

(1) As a general rule, funds should be invested as they accrue – there must be a very strong reason for delaying investment.

(2) A too-active policy of change may not be a good thing.

(3) High yielding stocks bought at a premium can to advantage be written down out of excess income with a view to eliminating the premium by the end of the term.

(4) Opportunities for favourable switches of British government securities should not be neglected. With large funds these switches can be very profitable. Here a leading stockbroker, well equipped with mathematicians, can be a great help. Sophisticated switching can be worth almost ½ per cent. more per annum on a gilt-edged portfolio.

(5) There is a good case for having an investment reserve to which incurred losses and realized profits can be transferred.

(6) The appointment of a trust corporation as custodian trustee of the funds' investments should be considered.

(7) A pension fund needs an investment expert either as investment manager to the fund or as a consultant; this apart from employing first class stockbrokers and seeking their advice. Alternatively, it can employ a firm of pension consultants and managers to supervise the investments of the fund and/or to administer and manage the fund, including the payment of pensions. I devote a whole book to pension fund investment which is published by Hutchinson & Co. under the title *Principles of Pension Fund Investment.*

CHAPTER 15

# Charities

CHARITIES cover the wide field of religion, education, care of children, cure of disease, moral welfare, the armed services, professional trade and other benevolent societies, refugees and aliens, old people, young people, animal welfare, and numerous other good causes.

It is impossible to estimate with reasonable accuracy the total number of charities or total charitable funds. Indeed a complete list of charities with even modest details of activities and assets would be a big contribution to the social history of England. According to the Charity Commissioners Report for the year 1972, there are 80,800 charities registered with the Charity Commissioners. Additionally, in October 1972 the responsibility for 22,000 mainly recreational charities was transferred from the Department of Education and Science to the Charity Commissioners, although some 10,000 educational trusts remained the responsibility of that Department. This total does not include subsidiary charitable funds within the main charity. The actual number of charitable trusts is much greater as the Churches, Friendly Societies, industrial provident societies, universities, British Museum and others are exempt from registration. The Nathan Committee in its most comprehensive report on charities estimated that charities numbered 110,000. I would now put the figure at 150,000.

As regards funds, £163 million by book values were held by the Official Trustee according to the Charity Commissioners Report for 1972. This does not include the charitable funds of £70·3 million (January 1973) held by the Charities Official Investment Fund, more generally known as C.O.I.F., which operates more or less on the lines of a unit trust.

The depositing of funds either with the Charity Commissioners or with C.O.I.F. is purely voluntary. In any case the larger charities would look after their own funds.

The income for example from the funds of the Church Commissioners for the year to 31st March, 1972, totalled £27,486,109 spread as follows:

| | |
|---|---|
| Stock Exchange investments .. | £13,374,658 |
| Real estate .. .. .. .. | £8,366,996 |
| Mortgages .. .. .. .. | £1,037,285 |
| Miscellaneous .. .. .. | £4,707,170 |
| | £27,486,109 |

The balance sheet value of all assets as at 31st March, 1972 was £434 million, and with a surplus of £100 million at market values disclosed for Stock Exchange investments alone the total of the Church Commissioner's assets could be of the order of £600 million, ignoring massive appreciation in real estate. Then there are the large funds of the Nuffield Foundation, the Gulbenkian Foundation and the like, not forgetting the vast number of almost moribund charities deficient in up to date objects and leadership, and lacking in the funds needed to secure efficient management. Thus it will be seen that the total funds of charities is pure guesswork, and the Nathan Committee did not hazard a guess. They are, in my view, well over £1,000 millions.

The Trustee Investments Act, 1961, was a shot in the arm for many charities. Until 4th August, 1961, the very large majority of them were limited to the fixed-interest stocks prescribed by the Trustee Act, 1925; most of these charities will have been in existence for fifty years or more, and all the time they have had to face a diminishing income in real terms. Many have been saved from extinction by seven-year covenanted donations.

Some of the larger charities have in various ways secured an extension in their powers of investment, mainly through applications to the court. As regards the majority limited to the statutory powers of investments, the freedom given by the Trustee Investments Act had for many come almost too late. The exercise of the new powers had almost certainly involved an appreciable drop in income. An abundance of 'jam tomorrow' is of doubtful worth if in the meantime the income is so reduced that there's not enough to pay the Secretary's salary. The investment problems of some charities will severely test the ingenuity of investment advisers. It is unfortunate for charities that the Trustee Investments Act does not permit trustees to purchase land, which is probably the supreme investment in an inflationary economy, and particularly suitable to a fund having a perpetual existence.

In considering the investment of charitable funds the following points have to be borne in mind:

(1) Charities are perpetuities.
(2) Charities are not subject to tax.
(3) Income is of supreme importance, as the large majority of charities cannot spend capital as income.
(4) A charity which has been limited to fixed-interest investments for many years has been able to do very little to combat the fall which has taken place in the value of fixed-interest investments and the loss of income purchasing power which has unfortunately gone with it. When fixed-interest stocks fall they fall more or less in harmony. Switches will provide only modest increases in income. Exchanges such as 2½ per cent. Consols into 2½ per cent. Treasury, 3½ per cent. War Loan into 3½ per cent. Conversion, and *vice versa*, will pick up only a helpful few points. Even skill of the highest order cannot stem the results of inflation or the effect of the depreciation in gilts where a fund has been restricted to fixed-interest securities for the last fifty years. There has indeed been very little room for manœuvre during the period of restriction to fixed-interest securities, other than endeavouring to spread maturity dates so that reinvestment will at least be spread and the dangers minimized of having to reinvest at times of low interest rates.

The principles of investment as set out in the earlier pages of the paper will of course be observed – in particular, the rule of going 'long' when interest rates are high and 'short' when low. I would, however, reiterate that the right time for investment is a matter for judgement, and how wrong the experts can be! But the opportunity to invest is available only when money comes in on maturity of stocks or as a result of selling lower coupon stocks as they approach maturity or as new money becomes available. Unfortunately, however, the bulk of charities do not receive a steady supply of new money.

The investment of charitable funds is often bedevilled by aged, inaccessible trustees who, when they are brought together, not infrequently disagree on investment policy. How difficult it has been up to five or ten years ago, for the expert on a board of governors in his endeavours to persuade his 'lay' colleagues to use their powers to buy equities where a charity had the powers. Charities are very much in need of daily expert advice and should not have to rely upon a financial committee which considers that it meets frequently if it meets once a quarter. A new look is essential in the case of the majority of charities if the new powers are not to be wasted.

Equities are, of course, very suitable for charities which have few commitments against capital and to which year-by-year appreciation and depreciation are of no consequence. Clearly, if there is ever a case for 100 per cent. in equities, charities make the case – assuming of course the trustees are expertly advised. Here I do not propose to repeat all the points I have stressed earlier, but a charity with full powers of investment should be ready to switch part of the fund from equities to fixed-interest and *vice versa* when conditions seem to cry out for such action.

Many of the charities which, as a result of the Trustee Investments Act, have power to invest 50 per cent. of their funds in equities will be under £10,000 in value; these trusts might with advantage obtain their equity quota through investment trusts or unit trusts.

The Charities Organization Investment Fund (C.O.I.F.) caters for the investment of charitable funds. This fund has full powers of investment so in theory it could invest its whole portfolio in equities. The fund has been going since 1963 and many charities transferred massive fixed interest portfolios to it. Because of this, up to the end of 1966 all that it had achieved was to invest on a 50/50 fixed-interest/equities basis. However, for a number of years they have accepted only cash where previously they accepted investments, and as a result of this and a determined effort to increase the proportion in equities, the fund in January 1973 held approximately 83 per cent. in equities, 13 per cent. in fixed-interest stocks and 4 per cent. in freehold properties. As most charities are restricted to the Trustee Investments Act, 1961, this is very satisfactory. Putting their funds with C.O.I.F. does give charities the chance of having a much greater participation in equities and also to have the benefit of the expert management of their funds. The Municipal & General has a special unit trust for the investment of charitable funds entitled 'Charifund', but the trustees are limited to investing the wider range fund (see page 152) in unit trusts.

CHAPTER 16

# Insurance and Assurance Companies

*Insurance Terms*

The term insurance is usually applied to fire, accident, motor and marine business and the four classes under the collective name of general business. Life business is usually termed assurance business and the companies which transact life business only as the life offices. Composite offices are those which undertake all classes of business including life. Companies owned by the shareholders are called proprietary companies and mutual companies are those owned by the policy-holders. There are recognized premium rates for fire risks and many accident risks. Those that abide by these rates are called tariff offices and those that do not are termed non-tariff offices.

*Extent of the Business*

The total premiums of the company members of the British Insurance Association for 1972 was £5,088 millions made up as follows:

| | £m. |
|---|---|
| Fire and Accident .. .. .. .. | 1,599 |
| Motor .. .. .. .. .. | 995 |
| Marine and Aviation .. .. .. | 268 |
| Ordinary Life .. .. .. .. | 1,895 |
| Industrial Life (door to door business) .. | 331 |
| | £5,088 |

My estimate for Lloyd's premium for 1973 is over £900 million – Lloyd's do not transact life business.

*Ownership and Extent of Funds*

There is considerable ignorance concerning the ownership of the funds of insurance and assurance companies. The funds are known to be vast; they total about £20,000 million, of which approximately £4,000 million are general funds and the balance (£16,000 million) life assurance funds. These are book values and the market values which are not disclosed are considerably in excess. What is not generally realized is the extent of the liabilities against these funds. In the case of insurance companies, the funds include provision for known outstanding general insurance claims, as well as reserves to cover unexpired risks which, for fire insurances, are normally a minimum of 40 per cent. of net premiums, for marine, a good deal more, and for accident and motor a minimum of 33⅓ per cent.

The £16,000-million life assurance funds form the security for the life policy-holders. In the case of mutual assurance societies the life policy-holders own the company. Where the company is owned by the shareholders, the shareholders are entitled to take only a share of the profits from life business. The amount of profit which the shareholders receive varies with assurance companies. It is usually more for industrial life business (door to door business) than for ordinary life business, where the average share of profits received by the shareholders is 10 per cent., the balance (90 per cent.) inuring for the benefit of the with-profit life policy-holders. The total funds of insurance companies, whether they be general funds or life funds, are not trusts in the normal sense of the word any more than the funds of any commercial or industrial company. The business of life assurance is certainly a quasi-trust, as the first concern of the directors in those cases should be the life policy-holders.

In contrast to general insurance funds, life assurance funds are not handicapped by having to keep 20 per cent. of their funds in overseas securities and, unlike the liabilities of insurance companies, the liabilities of life assurance companies can be reasonably accurately estimated by their actuaries. Further, the outgoings of life funds can, to a not inconsiderable extent, be financed out of incoming premiums and annuity considerations.

Life assurance companies must, however, invest their funds so as to maintain their values as, unlike pension funds, they must give careful attention to the year-to-year valuation of their securities. The actuaries are not likely to go very far wrong on their mortality estimates or on their calculations generally, but a substantial depreciation in the invested funds of an assurance company could endanger the bonuses payable to their with-profits policy-holders. It is well known that life assurance companies have been going into equities to a greater extent during the last ten years as compared with the past. The current figure would probably be slightly in excess of 37 per cent. of the book values of total life assurance funds, and at a guess 50 or more per cent. in market values. Thus at the present time the cushion of equity appreciation must be considerable, nevertheless the amount invested in equities must be carefully watched, as life companies must avoid the dangers to their funds arising from a 'bear' market in equities.

*Distribution of Life and General Funds*

The following shows the distribution for invested assets by book values of the funds at the end of 1972 of the life assurance and general funds of the company members of the British Insurance Association:

| | *Life* % *of total* | *General* % *of total* |
|---|---|---|
| Mortgages | 14·8 | 4·7 |
| British government and British government guaranteed securities | 17·2 | 8·0 |
| Foreign and Commonwealth government provincial and municipal stocks | 3·4 | 15·8 |
| Debentures and loan stock, preference and guaranteed stocks and shares | 17·6 | 19·5 |
| Ordinary stocks and shares | 28·6 | 35·6 |
| Real property and ground rents | 13·9 | 7·8 |
| Other investments | 4·5 | 8·6 |
| | 100·0 | 100·0 |

I would particularly point out the considerable investment in mortgages and real property. This book is, however, devoted exclusively to Stock Exchange investments, but there is a chapter on mortgage and property investment in another of my books, *Principles of Pension Fund Investment.*

The Radcliffe Report made the following appropriate comments on the investment of assurance company funds:

(i) 'In the investment of life funds "there is a broad bias in favour of matching liabilities with securities".'

(ii) 'Whereas normal practice is to invest the life funds in long-term investments, the general funds have to include a high proportion of readily marketable securities, including many short-dated securities whose market values are unlikely to suffer wide fluctuation.'

(iii) 'The inclination to commit the funds (assurance) at once to long-term investment does not imply that the bonds will be held to maturity. A long bond eventually becomes a medium bond, and a medium becomes a short. Their broad preference being for longs, the companies take opportunities, when markets seem favourable, to sell the bonds which have become short and reinvest in longs. . . .'

*Taxation and Investment*

Taxation has an important bearing on the investment of general (insurance) funds and the life funds of insurance and assurance companies. Insurance companies transacting general business are taxable, in broad terms, on interest plus or minus profits or losses respectively, including profits or losses on investments on their fire, motor accident, marine business, less of course expenses of running the business, *and* they pay at the current Corporation Tax rate.

The fact that profits on the sale of investments are taxed at a high rate must inevitably affect investment policy, as a company will tend to retain shares which show considerable appreciation even if otherwise it might reduce the holding and further diversify the portfolio. On the other hand, a company is encouraged to cut its losses. If, of course, it became highly desirable to sell a holding which would realize a substantial profit, it could be matched against a sale involving a corresponding loss. The credit for the loss can be used to offset other profits.

In the case of life assurance companies, annuity business is taxed on a different basis from other life business. Pension deferred annuity business was relieved of all tax by the Finance Act, 1956. Life business is assessed on interest plus profits less losses from investments less an allowance for expenses of management. Annuity business is taxed on profits. Both life and annuity fund business is subject to Corporation Tax, but by concession, at a maximum rate of 37½ per cent. which before decimalization was 7s. 6d. in the pound, which was the concession income tax rate.

It is not possible to do more than touch upon this very extensive subject of the investment of insurance and assurance funds. There are many learned papers on the subject which have appeared in the *Journal* of the Institute of Actuaries and the *Journal* of the Chartered Insurance Institute, but what has been written here may serve to correct one or two misunderstandings outside the insurance world.

*Insurance Shares as Investments*

Insurance companies are highly favoured, and rightly so, by investors. Nevertheless the investor, in a company which transacts life business, shares only modestly in the current prosperity of life assurance and, in the case of a composite office (a composite office being one which transacts both insurance and assurance business), substantial underwriting losses can be incurred on its fire, accident, motor and marine business. However, income from investments is substantial, and many offices distribute in dividends less than their actual interest earnings on their general funds.

Some financial papers have described insurance shares as 'investment trusts plus'. Without commenting on the relative merits of insurance companies and investment trusts as investments, I would regard the statement as an extravaganza. Insurance companies must keep a substantial proportion of their funds liquid as a provision against the catastrophe hazard associated with insurance, while those insurance companies transacting general business overseas have to lock up large funds in the countries in which the business is transacted – the figure could be as much as 20 per cent. of the book values of the total funds of insurance companies. Investment trusts invest up to 90 per cent. of their funds in equities. Insurance companies at present have 35 to 40 per cent. by market values of their total funds in equities – the figure when the Second World War began would have been in the region of 10 per cent. Nevertheless, the record of insurance shares as investments is absolutely first class. Dividends have increased by 8 per cent. per annum on average over the last ten years. The record of the life offices, and in these I include companies which mainly transact life business, has been outstandingly good.

General business is the risk business and because of this profits cannot be calculated accurately in advance. Apart from the last two or three years, the insurance companies transacting general business over the last decade have had very bad fire and motor loss experience with underwriting losses sometimes running into millions. However, these losses were struck before crediting any interest on the relevant insurance funds and the 'Yorkshire' only has reduced its dividend. The advent of Corporation Tax added another burden to the insurance companies but I expect that with some adjustment in their investment portfolios companies transacting general business will have more or less enough franked income to cover their unfranked income. Interest earnings have continued to increase at a satisfactory rate of approximately 10 per cent. per annum during the last ten years.

Life business has shown tremendous growth during recent years, premiums have grown from £983 million to £2,226 million in ten years. With life assurance, profit margins can be calculated with some exactitude. Skilled actuaries do their sums and allow for all the known hazards; mortality tables err on the side of caution and the result is almost bound to provide profit which grows as business grows. Although the shareholders of the proprietary offices only receive, as already mentioned, on average 10 per cent. of profits, the 10 per cent. is producing ever satisfactorily increasing amounts. Apart from all this the assets of the life companies are substantially greater than their disclosed book values.

The change to Corporation Tax hit the life assurance companies in as much as there was not enough franked income to cover increased dividends to their shareholders. The triennial of the Legal & General in respect of the three years ending 31st December, 1965 highlighted this. In the normal way investors would have expected the dividend to have gone up by 25 or 33⅓ per cent., but as the dividend had to be earned gross the best the Legal & General could do was to maintain the existing rate of distribution. It is thought in some quarters that it would take one triennial to overcome the handicap involved in the taxation change, and this is what happened.

Until the advent of Corporation Tax life assurance shares had certainly proved to be growth stocks of the highest order, with dividends increasing at the rate of 14 per cent. over the last ten years. In my view after a suitable pause the growth in dividends will continue more or less in keeping with the past record has been confirmed.

The following table will illustrate the worth of insurance companies as investments, better than any words:

VALUE OF £100 INVESTED ON 1ST JANUARY, 1952

| | *1.10.62* £ | | *1.11.66* £ | *20.9.73* £ |
|---|---|---|---|---|
| *Life Offices* | | | | |
| Legal and General .. | 1,806 | | 584 | 1,561 |
| Equity and Law .. | 1,566 | | 1,023 | 3,328 |
| Prudential .. .. | 314 | | 390 | 614 |
| *Composite Offices* | | | | |
| General Accident .. | 1,164 | | 809 | 1,129 |
| Eagle Star .. .. | 567 | | 336 | 876 |
| Northern .. .. | 356 | Later | | |
| Employers .. .. | 346 | Northern/Employers | 225* | — |
| Royal .. .. .. | 225 | | 220 | 401 |
| Phoenix .. .. .. | 167 | | 140 | 290 |

These figures have been supplied to me by a leading firm of stockbrokers specializing in insurance shares.

* Now in Commercial Union Group.

The table very well illustrates the effect of the imposition of Corporation Tax, as the second column of figures relates to a period just over a year after the tax commenced. The recovery since has been marked, but even so some offices have not got back to the values at 1st October, 1962.

CHAPTER 17

# Management and Supervision of the Personal Investments of Individuals

*Introductory*

Some institutions and investment consultants are prepared to help, with investment advice, individuals and others who are responsible as trustees for the investment of trust funds. The type of problem which the latter have to consider, and for which they rely upon the consultants for assistance, is set out elsewhere in this book under the heading of 'Personal and Family Trusts'. I am not here concerned with that type of problem. What I want now to consider is the supervision and management of the personal investments of individuals.

This type of service has been developed extensively in the United States; in fact, the individual who in this country would within the limits of his knowledge and time look after his own investments would, in the United States, automatically leave the work to a trust company and would give the company almost a free hand.

This service is not for the small man, who, before he invests in stock exchange securities, should have the maximum holding of National Savings Certificates (yield on current issue to maturity £5·7 per cent. free of tax), his appropriate life assurance cover, and possibly £1,000 in British Savings Bonds (current yield 8½ per cent. plus tax-free bonus after seven years of 3 per cent.) or the equivalent in building society shares (current interest 6·75 per cent. free of income tax at 30 per cent.). After that he can take an interest in equities through unit trusts or investment trusts.

*The Service*

The service of investment supervision is rapidly growing in this country, and it is now being fairly widely advertised by some institutions and small firms. At one time the appeal was addressed almost exclusively to the widow or spinster, who obviously needed some assistance with investments, and to the professional man who, preoccupied with his own profession, was neither able to acquire a knowledge of investments nor able to devote the time to their supervision. Today the appeal is to a much wider field, rather on the basis that no individual with his own job to do really has the time to give sufficient thought to his financial affairs. There is in fact every indication that even the knowledgeable investor finds he can do better working in collaboration with the investment department of a trust corporation or bank or investment consultant, sometimes called investment counsellor, teamed up with a leading firm of stockbrokers. In this way he avoids a tremendous amount of detailed work, much of it pernickety.

In publicizing the service the trust corporation indicates that it is prepared to supervise the funds and personal investments of individuals by means of a declaration of trust or an advisory trust – the terms are interchangeable. It is emphasized that the trust is not a fully blown trust, but merely an arrangement which is given effect to by a written agreement between the parties perhaps a mere exchange of letters; part of the arrangement usually involves the wise precaution of having the securities registered in the name of the trust corporation or its nominee.

The arrangement can be terminated on short notice by the depositor (the name sometimes given to the recipient of the service).

*Advantages*

Here are some of the advantages of the advisory trust service offered by trust corporations and others:

(1) Dividend dates are diarized and the collection of all income is assured. As a consequence no dividend is lost, as could easily happen when stocks are bought 'cum dividend' and not registered in time.

(2) An income remittance scheme is arranged by which the income is distributed to the depositor by fixed instalments monthly or quarterly. Provision can be made for payment of recurring charges, such as subscriptions or allowances. Once a year a statement is prepared giving full particulars of the portfolio of investments, showing in each case income (gross, tax and net received), payments made and the balance due. The totals give the depositor the information he needs for his tax return. With the statement is sent a cheque for the balance and, if

increased income justifies it, the periodic remittances are increased.

(3) The investments are supervised all the time and once a year (twice for large trusts) the investments are fully reviewed in conjunction with the depositor's stockbrokers.

(4) Although usually the investments are for convenience registered in the name of the trust corporation, no change is made without the consent of the depositor. The procedure is to make a recommendation after consultations with the stockbrokers. Reasons are given for the course suggested and the depositor has the opportunity of expressing his views. In this depositors will vary – some like to be consulted first, others prefer the trust corporation to carry through an investment change and to report it afterwards. In all cases there is provision for action in urgent cases without first referring. In my experience the depositor who gives his investment adviser full discretion does the best.

(5) The advisory trust service ensures that:

(a) an issue of rights is never overlooked: this can easily happen, particularly in the case of an individual who is travelling or who temporarily becomes too ill to handle his own affairs or who merely in the pressure of events overlooks the matter;

(b) every advantage is taken of a preferential right to apply for a stock, and in the same way the opportunity to make an application for excess shares is not overlooked. This is routine in a trust corporation's office; but an individual left to his own devices not infrequently fails to make use of application forms for preferential issues and excess shares, sometimes through lack of knowledge, occasionally through carelessness, and more frequently through lack of funds which often the trust corporation will advance temporarily;

(c) one very great advantage of the arrangement is that full details are kept of capital gains and losses which is a tremendous help to the depositor when making his tax return.

*N.B.* The service can be limited to investment advice and supervision of investments generally, the investments remaining in the name of the owner, with dividends mandated to his bank.

*The Operation of the Trust*

As in the case of an ordinary trust, the advisory trust might well start with the depositor sending a sum of money for investment; alternatively he will produce his current list of investments, in which case the first stage will be to review the list, following a similar practice to that outlined earlier. Where money only is provided at the commencement the adviser starts with a clean sheet and selects only investments which he fully approves. If, however, he has to start with the depositor's own investments, there is inevitably a good deal of cleaning-up to be done: this would include breaking down the depositor's prejudices in favour of certain of his investments which may be giving a high yield but which the adviser feels have little growth prospects. Getting an existing list straight therefore sometimes takes a few years, because the depositor cannot face up to a full-blooded operation in one 'go'.

Before an adviser can consider and make recommendations concerning an individual's investments, he must know, just as in the case of a life tenant of a personal trust, the circumstances of the depositor. The nature of the information required is set out under 'Personal Trusts' (page 111). It must be stressed, however, that the depositor, as owner of the fund, is both 'life tenant' and 'remainderman'. Obviously his total income apart from the advisory trust is of supreme importance in considering investments.

*Setting up the Fund*

When all the information relevant to the depositor's circumstances has been collected and recorded on his file, the first important decision to be taken, as in the case of a personal trust, is the proportion of the fund to be invested respectively in fixed-interest securities and equities.

Where the depositor has a substantial income it would be appropriate to select in the main, for the fixed-interest proportion, short medium-dated stocks standing at a discount – 3 per cent. Treasury Stock 1979, which is not subject to capital gains tax if held for one year; this type of stock is very suitable for someone paying income tax at a high rate. On the other hand, the depositor may be on the point of retirement and want to augment his pension as much as possible. Then it would probably be more appropriate to invest the bulk of the fixed-interest proportion in medium-dated to long-dated high-coupon stocks, even if standing at a premium. Treasury 9 per cent. 1994 at 98 gives a current yield of around 11·1 per cent., and it is the current yield in which this particular depositor will be interested. The problem of selecting fixed-interest stocks differs very little from those in the case of personal trusts (see page 116, and what is written under fixed-interest stocks on pages 17 to 34 should be noted).

If the depositor is deriving a satisfactory income from a position in a first class company, and it is certain that when he retires he will receive a substantial pension, it could be argued that he has already got his quota of fixed-interest income and that the bulk of his investments should be invested in equities. But, even in a case like this, there are occasions when the depositor will want a large sum of money, on changing house or to meet some unexpected commitment. Death duties also have to be borne in mind. Without question, selected money stocks are the best means of providing against likely commitments which cannot be timed.

Personally I feel it is inappropriate to have a 100 per cent. equity fund unless the depositor has the means of raising money in an emergency; in other words, unless he has the equivalent of fixed-interest stocks, such as life assurance policies, or can readily borrow money. Even borrowing money raises the question as to whether it would not be better to realize securities at that point of time. Incidentally, some trust corporations permit the depositor to borrow money temporarily against his advisory trust fund. Apart from all these considerations it might be appropriate to have a proportion of the fund in fixed-interest investment as a policy decision – the outlook for example of equities being uncertain or because there are signs of a falling off in trade.

Having taken into account the state of the equity market and in particular the individual circumstances of the depositor, it might be decided to set up the fund to begin with on a 50/50 basis, in which case the fixed-interest proportion could be as follows:

15 per cent. in short/medium-dated low-coupon British government securities;
15 per cent. in medium-dated British government securities;
20 per cent. in first class industrial debentures.

This percentage in fixed-interest stocks should leave plenty of elbow room to enable advantage to be taken of any substantial fall in the equity market or for entering into fresh investments through the usual attractive medium of rights issues.

As regards the 50 per cent. in equities the aim (as stressed on page 116 for the investment of family trust funds and on page 44 under 'Equity Groups') is to get as wide a spread of equities as possible through the various industries. For an equity fund of £50,000 or more, I would regard 3 per cent. of the total fund as the maximum for a giant blue-chip, 1½ per cent. for a medium-sized blue-chip, and 1 per cent. for a promising equity which is yet untried over a long term.

On the whole I favour securing equity diversification for the smaller funds through the purchase of investment trusts, although unit trusts must not be overlooked in this connection.

For the larger funds investment trusts should be considered as through them can be secured an interest in the vigorous growth of the United States. In any case, the professional investor will always be on the look-out for a reasonably priced investment trust share.

As already indicated the adviser will from time to time consider policy – whether, for example, to increase the percentage in equities or *vice versa*. It is unlikely, however, that a decision will be made to 'go liquid' on the whole fund. The dangers and difficulties of 'going liquid' are referred to on page 68, and 'going liquid' is not practicable where income is important. There are occasions, however, when the depositor will press his adviser to 'go liquid', and in such cases the latter will draw the attention of the depositor to all the difficulties (see page 69) and the depositor may be convinced that the operation is not worth undertaking. It is a decision for which the depositor must take responsibility: an adviser can only advise. This, however, does draw attention to one of the advantages of an advisory trust or any similar arrangement in that it introduces a 'buffer' (the adviser) between the depositor and his impatience; in fact, any financial expert will tell you that he wishes he could be as patient with his own investments as he is with other people's investments, and he will often aver that he does much better with other people's money than with his own – and I believe it. A compromise might be to 'go liquid' on 25 per cent. of the fund especially when current deposit rates are high or when short term British Government Stocks are suitable.

Once the fund has been set up, it will be reviewed in the normal way of not less than once a year.

PART 5

# Trustee Investments Act, 1961

CHAPTER 18

# The Act

*History*

The need for trustees to have power to combat inflation, so vigorously stressed in the Report of the Nathan Committee dated 31st December, 1952, was conceded at last.

The Trustee Investments Act became law on 4th August, 1961. It will go down in history as the Act which gave trustees power to buy equities. It contains many new features and all investors, not only those affected, should examine its provisions because it is in the nature of a guide to official thinking not only on trustee investment but on investment generally. Thus the struggle to liberalize the investment powers of trustees ended successfully – it is the only major change in the statutory investment powers of trustees since 1925 when the *Economist*'s consumer price index was 205 compared with 525 when the Act received the Royal Assent, and over 900 as I revise these pages. The final stages were set at a hot pace, the Report stage being completed on 13th July, back to the Lords on 31st July, Royal Assent 4th August. In the course of its progress through Parliament the Bill created much interest and it collected over 100 amendments with two major amendments accepted at the report stage.

This 'sprint' to get the Bill passed during a time when the Government was in the throes of a financial crisis with, among other things, divided limitation under consideration, is worth a passing thought; surely it means that despite recurrent financial troubles the Government still had faith in equities and wanted to give trustees the opportunity of buying them at the earliest opportunity – it would have been so easy to have postponed the Bill without giving any impression of postponing. Instead, at the last moment the Government accepted an amendment giving the Treasury power by order to increase the statutory power of trustees to buy equities up to 75 per cent. of the fund, subject to the approval of both Houses of Parliament. So far this additional step has not been taken.

The Act, which runs into twenty pages including its five schedules, is not easy to read and it shows signs of being rushed. Lord Conesford said in the House of Lords at the time that 'it is as nearly incomprehensible to a layman as an Act of Parliament can be'. It was urgent to give trustees power to buy equities on certain conditions, and many who had reservations on the Bill would rather have the Act as at present drawn than strive to perfect it at the expense of delays, and doubtless whatever disabilities emerge over the years will be put right by amending Acts.

*Investment Expert*

Whilst in very general terms the Government has kept fairly closely to the White Paper, the Act gives effect to a good deal of the criticism made during its passage through Parliament. This has resulted in greater discretion being given to trustees than originally intended and the dangers arising therefrom have to some extent been safeguarded by making it obligatory for trustees other than those who are themselves investment experts to obtain the *written authority* of an investment expert to changes in investments. The Act has rejected the White Paper's contentious definition of an investment expert, which gave rise to so many objections, and has defined an investment expert as 'a person who is reasonably believed by the trustee to be qualified by his ability in and practical experience of financial matters'. The definition is not without its imperfections.

The trustee also has to seek the expert's advice:

(a) as to the need for diversification of the investments of the trust insofar as it is appropriate to the circumstances; and
(b) as to the suitability to the trust of the investments (Section 6 (1) a and b);
(c) so long as any investments made in the exercise of the new powers given by the Act are retained the trustee must obtain advice on the lines of (a) and (b) above, from the investment adviser at such intervals as appears appropriate.

The advice has to be subsequently confirmed in writing.

The need to secure advice does not apply to one of two or more trustees where that trustee is the expert giving the advice to his co-trustee(s) or where the officer or servant of a trustee, who is competent to give the advice, exercises the powers of the trustee.

*Application of Act*

The Act applies to all trusts which before the passing of the Act had powers less than those granted by the Act – also to wills executed before the passing of the Act. It is possible, however, for a will or deed executed after the date of the Act to provide for powers less than those granted by the Act. The powers are in addition to a trustee's existing powers, not in derogation.

It must be remembered with this frequent reference to trustees that, to quote the long title, this is 'an Act to make fresh provisions with respect to investment by trustees and persons having the investment powers of trustees, and by local authorities and for purposes connected therewith'. Thus the Act applies to the superannuation funds of local authorities which are limited to statutory investments.

*Valuation and Splitting of Fund*

To obtain the new powers a trustee must have a valuation made of the trust fund and divide it into two equal parts, the narrow-range part, consisting exclusively of narrow-range investments, and the wider-range part. Part or all of the wider-range part can be invested in narrow-range investments but not *vice versa.* The division is a once-and-for-all division and thereafter the two funds have to be kept separate. Accretions, other than accruals to either part of the fund, are also subject to the 50/50 rule as are also appropriations of the fund. Distributions and payments out of the fund can be taken out of either fund at the discretion of the trustee.

*Special Fund*

A trustee with power to retain investments comprised in the wider definition and/or land can deduct their value before applying the 50/50 rule. If for example 20 per cent. is already in equities the balance (80 per cent.) can be invested as to 40 per cent. in the narrower-range investments and 40 per cent. (making 60 per cent.) in the wider-range investments. Generally the 50/50 rule will be applied to the proceeds of sale of special fund investments.

So much for the main principles of the Act.

*Scope of Investment Powers of Trustee Act, 1925*

Before setting out the new range of investments prescribed in the new Act it will be useful briefly to set out the statutory powers prescribed by the Trustee Act, 1925. Broadly these were:

- government stocks of the U.K.;
- securities the interest on which is guaranteed by the British government;
- certain Commonwealth and colonial government stocks;
- real and heritable securities in the U.K., including mortgages on freehold land;
- stocks in the Bank of England or Bank of Ireland;
- British Indian stocks and certain Indian railway stocks;
- certain stocks of public boards, county councils and municipal boroughs;
- certain prior stocks of the older public utility companies, such as railway, canal and water (with an ordinary dividend qualification);
- Northern Ireland government stocks; and
- any stocks authorized for investment of cash in the control of the High Court.

It will be noted that many of these investments have ceased to exist.

*The Prescribed Investments of the Act*

The new range of investments falls, as already mentioned, into two classes referred to as (a) the narrower-range investments, and (b) the wider-range investments.

Here are the narrower-range investments which in a sentence consist mainly of the 1925 Act investments plus debentures and unsecured loan stocks which are included for the first time:

### NARROWER-RANGE INVESTMENTS

PART I (not requiring advice)

1. Defence Bonds, National Savings Certificates, and Ulster Savings Certificates.

2. Deposits in the Post Office Savings Bank, ordinary deposits in a trustee savings bank and deposits in a bank or department thereof certified under sub-s. (3) of s. 9 of the Finance Act, 1956.

PART II (requiring advice)

1. Securities issued by Her Majesty's Government in the United Kingdom, the Government of Northern Ireland or the Government of the Isle of Man, not being securities falling within Part I of this

Schedule and being fixed-interest securities registered in the United Kingdom or the Isle of Man, Treasury Bills or Tax Reserve Certificates.

2. Securities the payment of interest on which is guaranteed by Her Majesty's Government in the United Kingdom or the Government of Northern Ireland.

3. Fixed-interest securities issued in the United Kingdom by any public authority or nationalized industry or undertaking in the United Kingdom.

4. Fixed-interest securities issued in the United Kingdom by the government of any overseas territory within the Commonwealth or by any public or local authority within such a territory, being securities registered in the United Kingdom.

References in this paragraph to an overseas territory or to the government of such a territory shall be construed as if they occurred in the Overseas Service Act, 1958.

5. Fixed-interest securities issued in the United Kingdom by the International Bank for Reconstruction and Development, being securities registered in the United Kingdom.

*N.B.* Fixed-interest securities are defined in the Act as securities which under the terms of issue bear a fixed rate of interest.

6. Debentures issued in the United Kingdom by a company incorporated in the United Kingdom, being debentures registered in the United Kingdom. Part IV supplemental to the Act gives the meaning of a debenture to include 'debenture stock and bonds, whether constituting a charge on assets or not, and loan stock or notes'.

7. Stock of the Bank of Ireland.

8. Debentures issued by the Agricultural Mortgage Corporation Limited or the Scottish Agricultural Securities Corporation Limited.

9. Loans to any authority to which this paragraph applies charged on all or any of the revenues of the authority or on a fund into which all or any of those revenues are payable, in any fixed-interest securities issued in the United Kingdom by any such authority for the purpose of borrowing money so charged, and in deposits with any such authority by way of temporary loan made on the giving of a receipt for the loan by the treasurer or other similar officer of the authority and on the giving of an undertaking by the authority that, if requested to charge the loan as aforesaid, it will either comply with the request or repay the loan.

This paragraph applies to the following authorities, that is to say:

(a) any local authority in the United Kingdom;
(b) any authority all the members of which are appointed or elected by one or more local authorities in the United Kingdom;
(c) any authority the majority of the members of which are appointed or elected by one or more local authorities in the United Kingdom, being an authority which by virtue of any enactment has power to issue a precept to a local authority in England and Wales, or a requisition to a local authority in Scotland, or to the expenses of which, by virtue of any enactment, a local authority in the United Kingdom is or can be required to contribute;
(d) the Receiver for the Metropolitan Police District or a combined police authority (within the meaning of the Police Act, 1946);
(e) the Belfast City and District Water Commissioners.

10. Debentures or guaranteed or preference stock of any incorporated company, being statutory water undertakers within the meaning of the Water Act, 1945, or any corresponding enactment in force in Northern Ireland, and having during each of the ten years immediately preceding the calendar year in which the investment was made paid a dividend of not less than 5 per cent. on its ordinary shares.

11. Deposits by way of special investment in a trustee savings bank or in a department (not being a department certified under sub-s. (3) of s. 9 of the Finance Act, 1956) of a bank any other department of which is so certified.

12. Deposits in a building society designated under 2. 1 of the House Purchase and Housing Act, 1959.

13. Mortgages of freehold property in England and Wales or Northern Ireland and of leasehold property in those countries of which the unexpired term at the time of investment is not less than sixty years, and in loans on heritable security in Scotland.

14. Perpetual rent-charges charged on land in England and Wales or Northern Ireland and free-farm rents (not being rent-charges) issuing out of such land, and in feu-duties or ground annuals in Scotland.

Now for the wider-range investments:

## WIDER-RANGE INVESTMENTS

1. Any securities issued in the United Kingdom by a company

incorporated in the United Kingdom, being securities registered in the United Kingdom which satisfy the conditions mentioned below.

2. Shares in any building society designated under s. 1 of the House Purchase and Housing Act, 1959.

3. Any units, or other shares of the investments subject to the trusts, of a unit trust scheme in the case of which there is in force at the time of investment an order of the Board of Trade under s. 17 of the Prevention of Fraud (Investments) Act, 1958, or of the Ministry of Commerce for Northern Ireland under s. 16 of the Prevention of Fraud (Investments) Act (Northern Ireland), 1940.

*N.B.* It will be noted that freehold and leasehold property is not included among the statutory investments of trustees.

The powers of investment set out above can be extended by Order in Council (s. 12).

*Further Conditions* – The following further conditions must be noted:

(1) Investments must be quoted on a stock exchange in the United Kingdom or the Belfast Stock Exchange.

But see 'Part IV Supplemental' para. 2 of the Act.

(2) Repayment of an investment must be in sterling.

(3) As regards shares and debentures they must
- (a) be fully paid up within nine months of issue; and
- (b) have been issued by a company incorporated in the United Kingdom which has
  - (i) a total issued and paid-up capital of not less than one million pounds;
  - (ii) paid a dividend on all its shares in each of the five years prior to the calendar year in which the investment is made.

*Generally*

(1) Local authorities are permitted to pool funds for investment in the form of unit trusts.

(2) The Court still has jurisdiction on application to increase a trust's powers of investment beyond the powers granted by the Act.

(3) The Act applies to trustees in England, Scotland, Wales and through Northern Ireland legislation to Northern Ireland.

## CHAPTER 19

# Comment on the Act

*Investment Advice*

The requirements of the Act will certainly demand all the skill of a trained and experienced investment expert and it follows that trustees must choose their investment advisers carefully. In my view expert investment advice is the cornerstone of the Act. It does appear that the Act rather points to getting a professional trustee who is himself an investment expert or who employs investment experts and I wondered whether this would result in trust corporations being appointed trustees in many more cases as they employ in their trustee departments trustee investment experts. There has been no dramatic increase in the appointment of trust corporations.

It will astonish some trustees to find that no investment other than Defence Bonds, National Savings Certificates, Post Office or Trustee Savings Bank Deposits can be made without securing the advice of an investment expert, whose advice must be confirmed in writing – unless of course the trustee himself is an investment expert or employs an investment expert. This has much to commend it as it ensures that the trust fund as a whole will have the benefit of expert advice which advice will, as already mentioned, have to be sought to ensure that the investments of the trust are as far as circumstances allow sufficiently diversified and suitable to the particular trust. As also mentioned, the trustee has to obtain and consider the advice of the expert at such intervals as appear to the trustee to be appropriate. The absence of any indication as to the extent of the intervals is a weakness although obviously a large fund would need attention more frequently than a small fund.

All this is to the good. It is the definition of an expert and the mechanics of carrying out all that has been referred to in the previous two paragraphs which I feel will give trouble. There is bound to be a difference of opinion as to who is 'a person who is *reasonably believed* by the trustee to be *qualified* by his ability in and practical experience of financial matters'. Surely someone clearly having first class experience in financial matters but no real experience in investment matters would not qualify. Again, it's the trustee who has to have the reasonable belief and there's going to be a vast difference in the conclusions of exercising that belief between an inexperienced lay trustee and an experienced trustee. The Court would, I feared, have to settle many a case brought by beneficiaries where disastrous results have followed from consulting the wrong kind of adviser. I elaborate on this in a chapter in *Purposeful Investment*, published by Hutchinson & Co., where I discuss the strange and imaginary case of Wilkins versus Charlie-boy. But so far there has been no rush to involve the Court.

Then on the mechanics of these transactions.

(1) In the past the majority of trustees have kept inadequate records. All this will have to end, because in self-defence the trustee will have to retain in a safe place all the written advice he has received – he may one day have to defend himself.

(2) I consider that the fact that a company has paid a dividend on all its shares in each of the five years prior to the calendar year in which the investment was made is no justification for its automatic choice. But once again it appears as if reliance is placed on the investment adviser to choose the right share.

(3) For a small trust diversification of equities is possible only through quality investment trusts or unit trusts.

(4) In the first edition, I warned that in the case of funds which are not subject to tax or beneficiaries under trusts who pay no tax or who are subject to tax at less than the standard rate, trustees should avoid equities and preference shares with a low net U.K. rate. Now following Corporation Tax and the end of the net U.K. rate the inexperienced trustee can no longer fall into this trap.

(5) The Act gives powers to the Court to extend a trustee's powers of investment beyond those set out in the Act. Prior to the passing of the Act many trusts secured powers greater than those in the Act by applying to the Court under the provisions of the Variation of Trusts Act, 1958. Much to the surprise of many investment advisers and myself, the judge a few years ago refused to give investment powers greater than the Act, taking the line that the Act laid down the appropriate investment powers of trustees (in *Re* Porritts Will Trust).

(6) As soon as the Act was published I wrote: 'I feel the Act is revolutionary in many ways – the legal recognition of an investment

adviser for one. This in my view will in due course lead to an Institute of Investment – the name is not important – and an examination qualification for investment advisers. I feel too that many of the professional examination bodies will in due course make room for a paper on the Art of Investment in their examination syllabuses. It is already possible to specialize in investments in the final Examination of the Institute of Actuaries. The same institute has an examination in investment for its Diploma in Investment. The Society of Investment Analysts awards a diploma by examination. The technique of investment is now one of the subjects covered by the recently instituted Stock Exchange Federal Examinations, success in which is necessary for membership of the Stock Exchange. The Fellowship examination of the Chartered Insurance Institute has a paper on investments. Examination will not make an Investment Adviser. No examination will give a man judgement or shrewdness but it is something to build these qualities upon – and it is agreed that the qualified man with experience is usually ahead of the unqualified man.' A Chair for Investment has been established in London at the new City University.

The Act brings to the light of day certain investment standards and it gives government blessing to trustees investing in equities. Diversification was a relatively unused investment term twenty-five years ago – now the Act has brought it into everyday parlance. The suitability of an investment, not just as an investment – but to the trust, is emphasized in the Act. The rival claims of life tenant and reversioner will have to be considered when an investment is made. 'Jam tomorrow is no use if the price is dry bread only today.' It is no use trustees of charities rushing in to buy blue-chip equities if the result is insufficient income to pay the secretary's already meagre salary. The typical finance committee which directs the investment policy of many a charity and other trust funds will have to streamline its activities if it is to succeed in the new investment climate.

A reliable investigation in the early sixties produced an estimated figure of £2,740 million of gilts held by trustees. Much of this money has gone into debentures and equities. My forecast that the Act must have a depressing effect on gilts and steadying effect on equities certainly materialized. In my view many trustees are still waiting for a rise in gilts and a fall in equities before taking full advantage of their new powers. Certainly in the twelve years since the Act there has been a steady and substantial fall in the prices of gilt-edged stocks while the trend of equities has been decidedly upwards, although these movements have in the main been caused by inflation and other factors.

Disenchantment with gilt-edged stocks has resulted in some trustees disposing of all gilt-edged stocks even on the narrow-range fund and obtaining an equity base in the narrow range by investing in convertible debenture and loan stocks. This move has served the funds very well and caused further pressures on gilt-edged stocks.

Nevertheless there seem times when gilt-edged stocks are attractive compared with equities, and the present could well be the time with the *F.T.* Actuaries twenty-year British Government Bond Index yielding over 12 per cent. to redemption, and the dividend yield on the *F.T.* Actuaries All Share Index giving a mere 4 per cent. Equities are admittedly well off their peak, but a difference of over 8 per cent. in favour of twenty-year gilts is strong food for thought. Indeed, in my view, it makes gilts more attractive at the present time for the medium term than equities.

APPENDIX I

# Suggested List of Equity Shares

THESE suggestions are made subject to the price being right at the time of purchase and in the case of cyclical stocks the time being ripe.

My personal preferences in each group are marked with an asterisk.

*Banks*

Barclays*
Lloyds
Midland
National Westminster
Hambros
Schroders
Mercury Securities

*Beer, Spirits and Minerals*

Allied Breweries*
Bass Charrington
Distillers
Guinness (Arthur)
Scottish and Newcastle Breweries*
Whitbread

*Building, etc.*

Associated Portland Cement*
London Brick
Ready Mixed Concrete
Redland
Rugby Portland Cement
Tunell Portland Cement
Taylor Woodrow
Wimpey (George)

*Chemicals*

Fisons
Glaxo
Imperial Chemicals*
Laporte Industries

*Discount House*

Alexanders Discount
Cater Ryder
Gerrard & National
Union Discount*

*Drapery and Stores*

Boots*
British Home Stores
Debenhams
Grattan Warehouses*
Great Universal Stores*
Marks and Spencer*
United Drapery
Woolworths

*Entertainment and Catering, etc.*

Associated Television
Granada
Grand Metropolitan*
Pontins
Rank Organisation*
Rediffusion*
Trust Houses Forte

*Electrical and Radio*

British Insulated Callender Cables
Decca
Electric & Musical Industries
Ever-Ready*
General Electric
Plessey
Thorn Electrical*

*Engineering*

British Oxygen
Brown (John)
Guest Keen & Nettlefolds*
Tube Investments

*Food*

Associated British Foods
Brooke Bond Liebig*
Cadbury Schweppes*
Fitch Lovell
Ranks, Hovis, McDougall
Reckitt & Colman
Sainsbury*
Spillers
Tate & Lyle
Tesco*
Unilever*

*Hire Purchase*

Mercantile Credit
United Dominions Trust*

*Insurance Companies*

LIFE OFFICES

Britannic
Equity & Law*
Legal & General*
Pearl*
Prudential*
Refuge
Sun Life*

COMPOSITE OFFICES

Commercial Union
Eagle Star*
General Accident*
Guardian Royal Exchange*
Phoenix*
Royal
Sun Alliance London

*Insurance Brokers*

Bowring C. T.*
Leslie & Godwin*
Sedgwick Forbes*
Staplegreen

*Investment Trusts*

Alliance*
Atlas Electric*
British Assets*
British Investment*
Cable & Wireless*
Foreign & Colonial*
Globe*
Industrial & General*
Mercantile*
Trustees Corporation*

to mention some of the larger but there are scores of good investment trusts.

*Mining*

Rio Tinto – Zinc

*Miscellaneous*

Beechams*
Hoover
Johnson Matthey
L. R. C. International
Metal Box*
Ozalid
Sears
Thomas Tilling
Turner & Newall

*Motor Trading and Aircraft*

British Leyland
Dunlop
Hawker Siddeley
Smiths Industries

*Newspapers*

Pearson Longman
Liverpool Daily Post

*Oil*

British Petroleum*
Burmah Oil
Shell*

*Paper*

Bowater
Dickinson-Robinson
Reed International

*Property*

Capital & Counties
Land Securities
Metropolitan Estate & Property

*Shipping*

British Commonwealth
Ocean Transport*
Peninsula & Oriental Steam Navigation

*Textiles*

Coats Patons
Courtaulds*

*Tobacco*

British American Tobacco*
Imperial Group

APPENDIX II

# A Selection of Debenture Stocks

| *Security* | *Size of issue* £ | *Price* | *Flat yield* £ | *Gross redemption yield* £ |
|---|---|---|---|---|
| Romney Trust<br>3% Debenture Stock<br>1970–80 | 100,000 | 64 | 4·62<br>(4·90) | 10·82<br>(7·74) |
| Imperial<br>(G.B. & I.)<br>4% Unsecured Loan<br>1975–80 | 20,000,000 | 62½ | 6·39<br>(5·65) | 11·90<br>(7·40) |
| Dunlop Rubber Company Ltd<br>4½% Debenture Stock<br>1972–82 | 10,651,000 | 62½ | 7·29<br>(5·95) | 11·91<br>(7·18) |
| English Electric Company Ltd<br>5½% Debenture Stock<br>1977–82 | 8,060,362 | 68 | 8·11<br>(6·47) | 11·46<br>(7·12) |
| Esso Petroleum Company Ltd<br>5½% Debenture Stock<br>1979–83 | 15,000,000 | 63½ | 8·77<br>(6·66) | 11·96<br>(7·30) |
| Gallaher Limited<br>6% Unsecured Loan<br>1983–85 | 10,000,000 | 63¾ | 9·48<br>(6·82) | 11·90<br>(7·18) |

| *Security* | *Size of issue* £ | *Price* | *Flat yield* £ | *Gross redemption yield* £ |
|---|---|---|---|---|
| Wilmot-Breeden (Holdings) Ltd 6½% Debenture Stock 1984–89 | 2,000,000 | 65 | 10·28 (7·35) | 11·60 (7·58) |
| Mecca Ltd 7% Debenture Stock 1985–90 | 3,500,000 | 65½ | 10·72 (7·33) | 11·73 (7·40) |
| Hepworth (J.) & Son Ltd 7% Debenture Stock 1986–91 | 1,000,000 | 64 | 10·76 (7·13) | 11·70 (7·16) |
| Unigate Ltd 7¾% Debenture Stock 1986–91 | 4,000,000 | 72 | 10·80 (7·30) | 11·48 (7·16) |
| Barclays Bank 8¼% Unsecured Loan 1986–93 | 59,000,000 | 73 | 11·62 | 12·13 |
| Associated Portland Cement 9% Debenture 1992/97 | 14,600,000 | 77¼ | 11·56 | 11·81 |
| B.P.B. Industries 10¼% Debenture 1997/2002 | 5,000,000 | 84xd | 12·02 | 12·10 |
| British Oxygen 11% Tonnage Debenture 1992 | 10,000,000 | 93¾ | 11·95 | 12·09 |

Prices and yields early September 1973 take into account interest and expenses. For comparative figures in brackets as at November 1966.

# Index